本书是江苏高校哲学社会科学研究项目
"现实与非现实故事人物对幼儿听读理解影响的眼动研究"的研究成果

在美华人家庭幼小衔接个案研究：
认知和参与视角

◎圣小利　著

Chinese Parents' Perceptions
and Involvement
in Their Children's School Readiness

南京大学出版社

图书在版编目(CIP)数据

在美华人家庭幼小衔接个案研究：认知和参与视角/圣小利著. —南京：南京大学出版社，2021.1
ISBN 978-7-305-23915-1

Ⅰ.①在… Ⅱ.①圣… Ⅲ.①学前教育-家庭教育-研究 Ⅳ.①G781

中国版本图书馆CIP数据核字(2020)第217591号

出版发行	南京大学出版社
社　　址	南京市汉口路22号　　邮编　210093
出 版 人	金鑫荣
书　　名	**在美华人家庭幼小衔接个案研究:认知和参与视角**
著　　者	圣小利
编　　辑	董　颖　　　　　编辑热线　025-83596997
照　　排	南京开卷文化传媒有限公司
印　　刷	江苏凤凰数码印务有限公司
开　　本	880×1230　1/32　印张 9.375　字数 210千
版　　次	2021年1月第1版　2021年1月第1次印刷
ISBN	978-7-305-23915-1
定　　价	50.00元

网　　址：http://www.njupco.com
官方微博：http://weibo.com/njupco
官方微信号：njupress
销售咨询热线：(025)83594756

* 版权所有，侵权必究
* 凡购买南大版图书，如有印装质量问题，请与所购图书销售部门联系调换

Acknowledgements

I would like to express my heartfelt thanks and humble appreciation to my committee, my family members, and my friends for the expertise, support, and encouragement that I have received before, during, and at the completion of the research project and dissertation.

Sincere appreciation is extended to my committee members: Dr. Evornia Kincaid, my committee chair, for her encouragement, enthusiasm, invaluable knowledge of current child development research, and dedication to young children; Dr. Jianjun Yin for his support and guidance in my life and study through all the years of my academic career at Jackson State University; Dr. Tony Latiker, Dr. Clifton Addison, and Dr. Kathy Bryant for their encouragement and the example of true scholarship.

I am grateful to my friends, Ye Yuan, Yali Hu, Yu Shi, Haiyan Zhou, and Li Zhai, for their faith, and faith in me. They inspired me and filled my working life with joy and creativity, and taught me about perspective throughout my journey. They also served as peer reviewers for the gift of their time and expertise.

I am blessed to be surrounded by family members who have supported my academic endeavors. Their belief in me has never failed, their love is the foundation for my life, and their courage has taught me about perseverance and hope in the midst of challenging circumstances.

Abstract

This qualitative study was to explore perceptions of Chinese parents about their children's formal school readiness in five domains, and to determine their involvement in their children's preparation for kindergarten guided by their belief through in-depth interviews with eight participants. The five domains consist of physical well-being and motor development, social and emotional development, approaches toward learning, language development, and cognition and general knowledge.

A case study approach examined school readiness perceptions from the perspectives of the participants and their involvement in children's preparation for kindergarten. Six themes emerged through analysis of transcribed interviews. They are parents' roles in children's school readiness, major factors effective in children's school readiness, parental involvement in children's school readiness, barriers in children's preparation for kindergarten, factors that affect Chinese parents' involvement, and suggestions concerning children's school readiness.

Conclusions were drawn from the findings of the study, associating with the areas explored by the research questions, and framed within the participants' perspective. They included the importance of school readiness, shifted values in parental perceptions, correlations between parental perceptions and involvement, reading and readiness, and suggested forms of parental involvement in children's school readiness. Implications linked the conclusions of the study to early childhood educators, to incoming Chinese parents, and to community sources, in consistence with the ecological system framework in the study. Future research efforts were suggested in emphasizing sample sizes and involving parents with various socioeconomic backgrounds in other places in the U. S. Data from children were also suggested in the future research. In addition, a longitudinal study was suggested so as to verify whether parental perceptions and involvement vary as children grow older.

Contents

Acknowledgements iii

Abstract v

Chapter 1 Introduction 1
    Background 2
    Statement of the Problem 6
    Purpose of the Study 8
    Significance of the Study 8
    Research Questions 10
    Delimitations and Limitations 11
        Delimitations 11
        Limitations 12
    Key Terms 13

Chapter 2 Literature Review 15
    School Readiness 16

Conceptualizations of school readiness ········· 16
Factors influencing children's school readiness
.... 18
Parental Perceptions ···································· 20
Parental perceptions and school readiness ····· 20
Parental Involvement ································· 26
Conceptualizations of parental involvement ········· 26
Parental involvement and school readiness ····· 28
Parental involvement and school readiness in
Chinese families in the U.S. ····················· 31
Theoretical Framework ································ 38
Social constructivist theory of child development
.... 38
Epstein's model of parental involvement ········· 42
The NEGP early childhood development
dimensions ··· 45

Chapter 3 Methodology ································ 49
Research Method ······································ 49
Research Design ······································ 50
Research Questions ···································· 54
Population ··· 54
Sampling ··· 55
Data Collection ······································ 59
Data Analysis ··· 61
Validity ··· 65
Reliability ··· 66

Chapter 4   Results ········· 68
Description of the Participants ········· 68
Findings ········· 75
 Theme 1: parents' roles ········· 77
 Theme 2: major factors effective in children's school readiness ········· 82
 Theme 3: parental involvement in children's school readiness ········· 96
 Theme 4: practices in conquering barriers in children's school readiness ········· 120
 Theme 5: factors that affect Chinese parents' involvement ········· 125
 Theme 6: suggestions concerning children's school readiness ········· 130
Summary ········· 134

Chapter 5   Discussion, Conclusions, Implications, and Recommendations ········· 136
Discussion of Core Themes ········· 137
 Theme 1: parents' roles in children's school readiness ········· 138
 Theme 2: major factors effective in children's school readiness ········· 139
 Theme 3: parental involvement in children's school readiness ········· 141
 Theme 4: practices in conquering barriers in children's school readiness ········· 144

　　　　Theme 5: factors that affect Chinese parents'
　　　　　　　involvement ·· 144
　　　　Theme 6: suggestions concerning children's
　　　　　　　school readiness ·· 145
　　Conclusions ·· 146
　　Implications ·· 153
　　　　Implications for preschool programming and
　　　　　　　kindergarten programming ·································· 153
　　　　Implications for incoming Chinese parents ··· 155
　　　　Implications for community sources ············· 157
　　Recommendations for future research ················ 157

References ·· 159

Appendices ·· 182
　　Appendix A: Cover Letter to Parents ··············· 182
　　Appendix B: Consent Form ······························ 185
　　Appendix C: Interview Questions and Prompts ······ 190
　　Appendix D: Healing Children's Trauma after
　　　　　　　Hurricane Katrina ·· 192
　　Appendix E: Dissertation Critique ······················ 212
　　Appendix F: Lesson Plan ······························ 224
　　Appendix G: Enhancing Pre-K in Mississippi ······ 242
　　Appendix H: Dissertation Evaluation ················ 277

Chapter 1

Introduction

It is school readiness that has been discovered to be a trustworthy benchmark of young children's academic success, social competence, and future adulthood development(Farver, Xu, Eppe, & Lonigan, 2006; Egertson, 1987; Shore, 1998; National Education Association, 2015). An increasing emphasis has been placed on young children's learning and could set the scene for all learning and life in the subsequent years of school and beyond. Early education clearly has an extensive positive effect on children. Several policy and programmatic efforts have been driven to improve young children's school readiness and ensure that they can master skills and knowledge upon their entry into formal schooling. Young children's school readiness skills are affected by multiple factors consisting of high-quality childcare programs, family environment, the neighboring community, and different aspects of parenting(Rosenkoetter, Schroeder, Rous, Hains, Shaw, & McCormick, 2009). Parenting, one of these determinants, exerts an important role in young children's cognitive, emotional, and social development (Bronfenbrenner, 1986; Rosenkoetter et al., 2009).

School readiness skills include the qualities and skills that a young child has upon entry into kindergarten. This chapter provides an introduction, and an overview of this study on Chinese parents' perceptions and involvement in their children's school readiness and preparing their children for kindergarten.

Background

The Asian population in America had advanced from 2.8% of the total population in 1990 to 5.28% in 2013, according to U.S. Census Bureau (2016) statistics. Approximately 50.6% of Asian Americans have earned a bachelor's degree or higher level of education, compared with 30.1% for all Americans (U.S. Census Bureau, 2016). An increasing number of Asian visiting scholars and international students have come to America to pursue and further their education. This group of parents holds a master's or higher degree. Asian families value the traditional view that academic achievement is the primary predictor of a child's future success. Confucian values and principles dominate traditional Chinese culture, which deeply influences the parenting in Chinese families. Parental training of children, parental authority, and filial piety are prevalent in

Chapter 1 Introduction

Chinese families(Chao, 1994). Hence, Chinese parents tend to exert more directive and controlled behavior over their children than other racial groups (Jose, Huntsinger, Huntsinger, & Liaw, 2000).

The immigration from China to the United States was initiated in the 1800s. They were among the earliest immigration groups in America. Even though less than 50 Chinese people lived in the United States before 1850, the discovery of gold in California around 1848 triggered a sharp increase in the number of Chinese immigrants(Wong, 1995). According to Siu (1996), the number of Chinese immigrants in the United States grew very slowly at first, and Chinese Americans are relatively newcomers compared to other ethnic groups. After the Immigration Act of 1965, there was a surge in the number of Chinese immigrants (Tsai, 1992; Wong, 1995). The foreign-born Chinese Americans are from various parts of the world with the Chinese descent: China and Singapore, but some have come from other places; the majority of them speak Mandarin Chinese, Cantonese, and Toisanese. Many Chinese, as well as other Asians, preferred to reside on the west coast or northeast region of the United States. There were a limited number of Chinese families living in the southern United States. As a result, the research on young children's school readiness among the population of Chinese families was worthwhile.

The research of Okagaki and Frensch(1998) on

parenting and children's academic achievement found that Asian American parents tended to set a high standard for their children's academic achievement, compared with European, American, and Latino parents. Asian students, including Chinese Americans and Chinese, generally earned higher academic success than their counterparts from other backgrounds. The efforts of Chinese parents in preparing their children for kindergarten, to a larger extent, resulted in their excellent performance in school(Zhao & Qiu, 2009). However, apart from the development in the cognition and general knowledge, Chinese parents provided little response to other domains of school readiness development. This was especially true for the international students and visiting scholars with young children born in China; some of them had no access to English prior to their learning in the United States. As a result, the investigation of Chinese young children's school readiness in multiple domains is needed.

Transitioning to kindergarten marked a critical period for young children as they embarked on the journey of formal schooling. Upon entry to kindergarten, young children were confronted with higher expectations of independence and responsibility as well as higher demands for social and academic skills(Rimm-Kaufman, & Pianta, 2000). The formal schooling posed a variety of challenges for children involved in cognitive, social, and emotional transformations(Pianta & Cox, 1999). Researchers believed

Chapter 1 Introduction

that having a smooth adjustment and transition in these areas was of great value because they were positively related to children's later school outcomes (Hair, Halle, Terry-Humen, Lavelle, & Calkins, 2006; Petrakos & Lehrer, 2011).

Parents are the first teachers of young children and dedicated to nourishing, protecting, and guiding their children in order to promote positive development and socialization(Brooks, 2011). Desirable and effective parenting is conducive to developing children's basic skills and appropriate moral sense [National Association of School Psychologists(NASP), 2006]. A multitude of studies have been conducted to examine the impact of parenting on children's school outcomes.

The effects of parental involvement in children's school outcomes have been well-documented (Swick, 2007). The involving of parents in their children's education and development induced positive benefits, including enhanced motivation(Green, Walker, Hoover-Dempsey, & Sandler, 2007), better academic outcomes (Hoover-Dempsey, Battiato, Walker, Reed, Dejong, & Jones, 2001), school attachment (Grolnick, Friendly, & Bellas, 2009), and fewer discipline problems and better social adjustment (Epstein & Sheldon, 2002).

With regard to young children and their parents, kindergarten is a crucial period when the challenge of adapting to the school environment comes into being. High school readiness was believed to have been increased by the likelihood that young children were successful in kindergarten, and later in elementary and high school(Entwisle, 1995). The No Child Left Behind Act of 2001 exemplified the emphasis on academic skills and literacy as early as kindergarten(No Child Left Behind Act of 2001, 2002). Unfortunately, not all preschoolers were fully ready for a school environment, which could have exerted a negative influence on their long-term success in school. Parents in the United States attached much importance to the transition of their children from preschool to kindergarten, and Chinese parents were no exception. Chinese parents struggled to prepare their children for kindergarten in various domains of young children development.

Statement of the Problem

School readiness and preparing children for kindergarten has increasingly become the pivotal issue among teachers and parents. School readiness skills include five domains of children development: physical well-being and motor development, social and emotional development, approaches toward learning, language development, and cognition and general knowledge [National Education Goals Panel(NEGP), 1995]. Head Start (2011) stated that school readiness appropriate for ages and development of enrolled children includes five domains: language and literacy, cognition, approaches to learning, physical health and motor development, and social and

Chapter 1 Introduction

emotional development. Children were expected to attain predetermined levels of social development and academic competence upon their entry into formal schooling. Failure in cognitive, language, and social-emotional competencies have been examined as predictors of poor performance in school(Justice, Bowles, Pence, Turnbull, & Skibbe, 2007). Even though there is sufficient evidence to unfold that family factors influence children's school performance over and above school influence (Brofenbrenner, 1986; Eccles &Harold, 1996; Fan & Chen, 2001; Hill & Taylor, 2004; Stone, 2006), limited research exists on parental perceptions and involvement in children's school readiness, especially in Chinese family settings. Further studies are needed to explore parental perceptions and involvement in the school readiness skills of younger children in various domains. It has been studied that Chinese students are better prepared for the academic rigors of kindergarten learning(Huntsinger et al., 1998; Schneider & Lee, 1990; Tsai, 1992).

The central problem that this study addressed was to explore perceptions of Chinese parents about their children's formal school readiness in five domains, and to determine their involvement in their children's preparation for kindergarten guided by their belief.

Purpose of the Study

Parenting and familial cultural beliefs do play a crucial role in promoting young children's attitudes, knowledge, and skills linked to education (Kim, Im, Nahm, & Hong, 2012; Trumbull & Rothstein-Fisch, 2011). The contribution of parenting to the education and development of young children includes a complex process. The mixed findings in the literature on parental perceptions and involvement across cultural groups suggest the need to investigate parental perceptions and involvement in children's school readiness in non-Western populations.

The purpose of this study was to probe the attitudes and motivations of Chinese parents and their practices to prepare children readiness for kindergarten in a southern city of the United States. A thorough understanding of the principles can afford caregivers, parents, educators, and policy makers with insight regarding how early parenting contributes to young children's successful entry into kindergarten.

Significance of the Study

This study will make a crucial contribution to education improvement because it will allow educators and parents to adjust their attitudes, motivations, and practices regarding

Chapter 1 Introduction

young children's school readiness. Research in early childhood education in Chinese families is still a relatively new and developing field (Xu, 2005). Since parenting is affected by social-cultural structures and cultural values, it was necessary to explore the feasibility of the application of Western theoretical and empirical research findings in Chinese cultural settings. Some researchers (Hirschman & Wong, 1986; Stevenson et al., 1985) have conducted studies on Chinese families and their children's high academic achievement, and explained their success was tightly linked to traditional Chinese cultural values. Little research has been conducted on Chinese parents' perceptions of their children's school performance during the transition from preschool to kindergarten. The study of parental perceptions was of great significance for researchers, teachers, parents, and children themselves; parental perceptions guided their behaviors at home. According to Walberg (1984), parents' behaviors at home called "the curriculum of the home" influenced the children's education and development considerably better than the socioeconomic status of families. Additionally, this study contributed to the dearth of literature regarding parental perceptions and involvement in children's school readiness in a Chinese population.

This study promoted the awareness of the importance and necessity of parental involvement in children's education and development among parents and educators.

School administrators and teachers developed parental training programs, and supplied other educational services and resources to assist parents in building desirable parent-child interaction, and facilitated young children's smooth transition to kindergarten. The results of this study potentially benefited educational practitioners who were eager to understand why Chinese children can enter kindergarten with such a high level of school readiness. In this way, the educators could carry out activities in order to highlight the achievement motivation of the students (Trumbull & Rothstein-Fisch, 2001). In addition, this study can inform educators about the specific Chinese educational practices to help improve non-Chinese students' academic achievement as early as kindergarten, and assist educators working with Chinese students to better understand their cultural practices, values, and beliefs. What's more, parents of non-Chinese students may learn something from Chinese parents' educational practices to better prepare their children for kindergarten.

Research Questions

The main issue of this study was to explore how Chinese parents perceive their children's school readiness in the academic domain, and to find out whether cultural and linguistic factors could enable Chinese students to achieve high academic success upon entering kindergarten. The following research questions guided this study.

1. How do Chinese parents perceive their role in their children's school readiness and preparation for kindergarten?
2. What are the major factors Chinese parents consider to be effective in their children's school readiness and preparation for kindergarten?
3. What are strategies and practices that Chinese parents employ in their children's school readiness and preparation for kindergarten?
4. What are the factors that affect Chinese parents' involvement in their children's school readiness and preparation for kindergarten?

Delimitations and Limitations

Delimitations were selected on purpose to concentrate this study on Chinese students at a single southern city of the United States. Limitations out of the researcher's control were taken into account across this study. The limitations in connection with this study, as were with many qualitative studies, are in linkage with the accuracy of responses from the participants and the limited number of samples.

Delimitations

This study was delimited by choosing a convcniene

sample. The focus of this study was laid on Chinese students attending schools in one southern city of the United States. The acute emphasis on this specific location sprang from the social relationship of the researcher with Chinese families in the community and the connection with the schools' leaders and personnel. The delimitation has provided Chinese parents and school officials to directly meditate on the results of the study owing to its proximity. The inquiry occurred over an approximate three months.

Limitations

Natural conditions that may have influenced the results of this study consisted of approaching the participants, and accuracy of the participants' responses. In spite of the fact that the researcher has already made great efforts to create a comfortable atmosphere for open and truthful participation, it was hardly possible for the researcher to guarantee the sincerity and willingness of the participants to uncover personal familial information during the interviews. Factors beyond the researcher's control involved the participants' ability to correctly recall and display activities or practices that they employed to enhance their children's skills and knowledge during the transition from preschool to kindergarten. The adoption of a small sample from a southern city in the United States, to some extent, restricted generalizability to other similar settings.

Chapter 1   Introduction

Key Terms

For the sake of understanding frequently-used terminology in this study, the following definitions of key terms were provided:

School Readiness. There is no consensus of the definition of school readiness. In this study, it is defined as children's sufficient preparation for entering formal school to engage in and benefit from learning experiences in kindergarten with interactions among people, settings, and institutions(Mashburn & Pianta, 2006).

School Readiness Skills. School readiness skills include the qualities and skills that a young child has upon entry into kindergarten. They are a combination of qualities and skills in (a) physical health and wellbeing, (b) social competence, (c) emotional maturity, (d) language and cognitive development, and (e) communication skills and general knowledge(Janus & Offord, 2007).

Parenting. Parenting refers to the values, attitudes, and practices of parents in their children's education and development.

Parental Involvement. Parental involvement stands for parents' active engagement in every aspect of their children's education and development(Jeynes, 2007). Parental involvement consists of multiple parents' behaviors including volunteering in school activities, helping with children's homework, discussing with children regarding school events, and actively participating in the school's decisions and policies.

Child Development. *Mosby's Medical Dictionary* (2009) indicated that child development is the diverse phases of social, physical, and psychological growth that happen from a child's birth through young adulthood.

Chinese. Chinese in this study refers to Chinese immigrants, visiting scholars, and international students in the United States of America.

Parent. Parent refers to the parent, step-parent, or guardian who was a primary caretaker of young children. The young children must have lived primarily in the home of the participating parent/guardian, and the participating parent/guardian was the most knowledgeable about the education and development of the child (National Household Education Survey School Readiness Survey, 1993).

Chapter 2
Literature Review

The examination of Chinese parents' perceptions and involvement in their children's school readiness took place from various theoretical perspectives and diverse disciplines. Chapter 1 contained a summary of a qualitative case study examining Chinese parents' perceptions and involvement upon their children's entry into kindergarten. Chapter 2 included a literature review on studies in relation to parental perspectives and involvement in school readiness in relationship to the current research. The literature review consisted of five sections, the first of which reviewed school readiness followed by school readiness of Chinese children in the United States. The third and fourth sections examined Chinese parental perceptions and parental involvement. The final section discussed the theoretical framework of this study. The theoretical basis of this study consisted of theories regarding parental perceptions and involvement in school readiness. The theoretical framework included Social Constructivist Theory of Child Development, Epstein's Model of Parental Involvement, and National Education Goals Panel Early Childhood Development Dimensions and the National Governors' Association.

School Readiness

Conceptualizations of school readiness

The conceptualization of school readiness in the United States of America originated in 1989, when President George Bush initiated the National Educational Goals Panel (NEGP). One of the educational goals mandates that while young children enter kindergarten, they should get ready to learn (NEGP, 1995). Afterwards, the notion of school readiness became one of the focuses of scholars, educators, policymakers around the world (Rafoth, Buchenauer, Crissman, & Halko, 2004; Zhang, Sun, & Gai, 2008). In spite of its pivotal importance, there was still no consensus among early childhood education researchers and professionals regarding the conceptualization of school readiness (Kagan, 1992; Rafoth, Buchenauer, Crissman, & Halko, 2004). For instance, Graue(1992) ascertained that school readiness of children consisted of all developmental domains rather than hinging on the single aspect of prerequisite academic skills or developmental maturation.

The NEGP extended the conceptualization of school

Chapter 2 Literature Review

readiness to five main developmental domains, including physical well-being and motor development, language development, social and emotional development, cognition and general knowledge, and approaches to learning (Kagan, Moore, & Bredeka, 1995). Physical well-being and motor development refers to children's physical development, health status, and physical abilities. Poor health status may result in frequent absences from school and increase the risks of failure in acquiring academic skills, and discourage further academic advancement. Additionally, physical health consists of age-appropriate motor skills, physical coordination, and energy levels to take part in school activities.

Social and emotional development relates to children's capability to communicate their feelings and socialize with adults and peers. A socially competent child is able to develop and maintain friendships, solve conflicts, appreciate differences, and function effectively within groups. Highlights of this domain act as a foundation for children's future school success and meaningful life experiences. Approaches to learning included enjoyment of learning, curiosity, creativity, confidence and reflection, attention to task, and interests and attitudes. Language development means that children master verbal expression, emergent literacy, and understanding skills to interact with others effectively. Cognition and general knowledge incorporates basic knowledge of concepts and the workings of the environment, cognitive competencies like early mathematical skills, and basic problem-solving skills. Although the five domains are distinct and separate, there exists a constant overlap of skill learning in early childhood development. Children have diverse cultural backgrounds with unique life experiences and ability levels. It is anticipated that children may display competencies in individual ways and show various patterns of development.

In accordance with NEGP, school readiness has a broadly scoped definition involving physical, social-emotional and cognitive readiness. Hence, school readiness is conceptualized as a young child's attainment of a set of behavioral, emotional, and cognitive skills needed to work, learn, and function successfully in kindergarten (Rafoth et al., 2004) in the current study.

Factors influencing children's school readiness

It is expected that children can perform well upon entering formal schooling, mastering predetermined levels of social development and academic competence. If children fail in school readiness and preparation for kindergarten, any early gaps may become wider throughout the child's further school career(Aunola, Leskinen, Lerkkanen, & Nurmi, 2004). Among the factors affecting children's school readiness, the family system has been figured out as one of the most influential one in predicting children's development outcomes(Bronfenbrenner, 1992).

Chapter 2　Literature Review

For instance, Coleman(1966) put forward strong evidence to support the notion that compared with school, family background and environment exerted more effects on children's academic performance. Within a family context, a nurturing environment may enhance children's cognitive, physical, and socio-emotional development (Mehaffie & Fraser, 2007). In addition, McWayne, Cheung, Wright, and Hahs-Vaughn (2012) indicated that positive parent-child interaction has been essential to children's achievement in academic and social development. It could be concluded that parenting exerts great impact on children's development and their adjustment to school. Parental perceptions and parental involvement guided by their perceptions stand for two prominent elements in the process of child-parent interaction; and both conduce to children's acquisition and development of school readiness skills.

Apart from parenting, an array of other demographic factors also influence children's formal school readiness, such as parents' educational level, family income, family structure, and child's gender, and so on. In the study of Janus and Duku(2007), the gender was one of the determinants with linkage to children's school readiness and boys were found to be more vulnerable to the problems than their girl peers. Family structure was revealed to be an important predictor of children's readiness skills. Children from single or no parent families are likely to have school problems like hyperactivity(Kerr, 2000). Children whose parents have low educational levels demonstrate poorer performance in math and reading skills than their peers with higher educated parents(West, Denton, & Reaney, 2000). It was also discovered that children from middle or high-income families have stronger social competence and better approaches to learn skills than those from low-income families. According to a recent study(Wang, Li, & Li, 2014), Chinese children's parental educational level and household income exerted a great impact on their performance in mathematics. The negative influences of demographic risk factors, however, can be moderated by active parental involvement(Kingston, Huang, Calzada, Dawson-McClure, & Brotman, 2013). These researchers found that parental involvement attenuated the relations between family structure and young children's socio-emotional development. Considering the important role of demographic factors in children's readiness for school, child sex, parental educational levels, family income, and family structure will be used as control variables when examining the effects of parenting on children's acquisition of school readiness skills.

Parental Perceptions

Parental perceptions and school readiness

While school readiness has been identified or interpreted in many different ways, little research has been conducted to explore the parental perceptions upon this topic(McAllister

Chapter 2   Literature Review

et al., 2005; Pianta & Kraft-Sayre, 1999). In a qualitative study of McAllister el al. (2005), primary caregivers were interviewed and asked to talk about (a) how they think about children's learning, (b) what they think is the meaning of school readiness, (c) what they think entering kindergarten would be for their child, (d) what is their role in helping their child's transition into kindergarten, and (e) how the community and policies influence school readiness. From their feedback, it was found that parents discussed more about their role and practices at home in their child's education but rarely about their engagement in their child's school activities. And they regarded emotional health and social skills as crucial factors for their school readiness. Many parents believed that it was of importance to discuss with their child regarding schooling. Parents relied on friends, relatives, programs like Head Start, and other support systems to help prepare their child for kindergarten.

According to a survey by Pyle, Bates, Grief, and Furlong(2005), about parents' perceptions of their children's formal school readiness, their knowledge of the educational systems, their comfort level of access to school services, and interaction with school personnel indicated that children obtained greater success in school when the interactions between the parents and the school were positive, and their parents were involved in their children's development. The study conducted by Seligman(2000) unveiled that parents' attitudes regarding their own school experiences exerted a great effect on their children's attitudes about kindergarten and school. That is to say, parents who express their negative feelings with respect to teachers or school can influence their children's success in school. Nevertheless, the mindset of the parents can be adjusted if their children have positive experiences at school (Olsen & Fuller, 2012).

According to a study by the PNC Financial Services Group, Inc. (2007), there was a difference between parents' and teachers' perceptions about school readiness skill development upon kindergarten entry. Among a population of 1,001 parents with young children age 8 or younger, and 516 teachers, approximately 80% of the parents ascertained that their children were socially ready for kindergarten; less than 15% of the kindergarten teachers agreed. Cognition skills consisted of identifying and sorting objects, recognizing basic counting and numbers, recognizing common words or signs, and reading and writing the alphabet. Regarding this domain, only 25% of the parents believed that their children were prepared for kindergarten.

Piotrowski et al. (2000) found that parents attached more importance on academic readiness skills, including knowing numbers and letters, while teachers placed more emphasis on behavioral skills such as listening and sitting still. It was also indicated that both parents and teachers

Chapter 2 Literature Review

approved that children should be socially competent, healthy, and able to follow rules. Researchers Lin, Lawrence, and Gorrell (2003) found in their longitudinal study that teachers valued children's social aspects of development more than their academic skills. Teachers' school readiness expectations were affected by the child's gender, age, and geographic region. Overall, parents viewed their child as academically and socially prepared for kindergarten based on their role at home, or their child's participation in a preschool program. Teachers viewed students as less prepared academically and socially when they started kindergarten, and valued behavior skills more than academics skills. Perhaps the variance in parents' and teachers' perceptions was due to the parents' unawareness of the kindergarten curriculum and expectations.

Parents have a variety of beliefs regarding what qualities their children will embrace to succeed in kindergarten, and what are the practices they should conduct in their children's development. Parental perceptions on school readiness are critical because parental beliefs exert influences on the programs, activities, and practices they arrange for their children (Graue, 1992). Parents evaluate their children's school readiness upon entry into kindergarten based on their perceptions, so their children will profit from their kindergarten experience (Westet et al., 1993). The National Center for Education Statistics (NCES) is the primary federal entity with the purpose of fulfilling a congressional mandate to have reports on the condition of education in the United States of America(NCES, 2010).

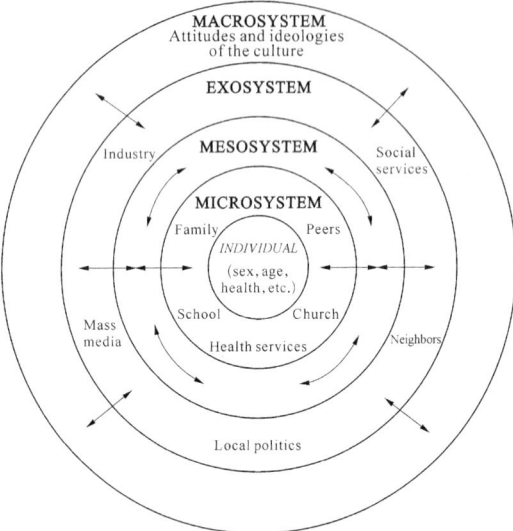

Figure 1 Bronfenbrenner's social ecology model of human development

Bronfenbrenner's social ecology model of human development, which is shown in Figure 1, underlines the potential for direct impact from the family(Mesosystem) to a child (microsystem). And the parent participation is clearly an attribute in a quality education. However, there is variation in parents' perceptions regarding school readiness. Both parents and other family members can have a wide range of perceptions of what attitudes and attributes their children need to possess in order to succeed in their kindergarten(Kim et al., 2005). Parental perceptions have effects on the activities they will engage in with their young children, the experiences they will schedule for their children, and the way they will prepare their children for formal schooling(Graue, 1992; Yeboah, 2002). The initial transition to kindergarten is a major change in a young child's life and can be one of the most uncertain, difficult, and confused stages. Children are able to adapt quickly to the kindergarten environment, build confidence, and maintain self-reliance and self-esteem with their parents' assistance(Yeboah, 2002).

Parents who believe themselves as more effective tend to be more engaged in their children's education. In a study conducted by Pelletier and Brent(2002), parent factors and teacher strategies were examined in fostering parent involvement in a preschool program. They found that preschoolers' parental perceptions of self-efficacy consisted of: (a) their own teaching efficacy on the basis of their instructional skills and the influences in academic, social and motivational domains on their children, (b) their perceptions about who influences learning, and (c) the degree of confidence they have. Pelletier and Brent(2002) came to the conclusion that parents are crucial in the educational phase and that they are more willing to become involved in their children's preparation for kindergarten when they perceive that they have the ability to effectively influence their children's education. Parents' active participation is a positive way to support their young children's school readiness.

According to Nelson(2005), a child's approach to

learning is key in their school readiness. Intrinsic motivation to learn is developed together with a sense of confidence and independence. Young children with this internal sense of confidence will persist with academic challenges and make great efforts to acquire new concepts. The parents are encouraged to model the behavior and assist their children to gradually develop independence and self-confidence.

Parental characteristics like levels of engagements and communication in home reading activities were found out to be linked to children who acquire more readiness indicators (Brooks-Gunn & Markman, 2005). Graue et al. (2003) conducted interviews with 14 parents in relation with their perceptions about readiness, and indicated that these parents held strong beliefs in an age-based readiness model for kindergarten. Marshall(2003) clearly stated in his study that the concerns about readiness from parents are often based on outdated assumptions and beliefs regarding the meaning of readiness.

Parental Involvement

Conceptualizations of parental involvement

With regard to the definition of parental involvement, numerous scholars and researchers have provided different versions. Maccoby and Martin(1983) defined parental involvement as the degree to which the parent is engaged to his or her role as a parent and to the fostering of a young child's development. Grolnick and Slowiazek(1994) referred to parental involvement as the level of parents' devotion to their children's education-related life. Other researchers regarded it as a multifaceted notion consisting of a variety of parental practices (Epstein, 2001; Ho, 1995). In this current study, parental involvement is conceptualized as the specific techniques or practices of parents in order to facilitate their children's development and education(Fan & Chen, 2001). These specific parental techniques and practices involve assisting children with homework, reading to children, volunteering at school, and interacting with teachers regarding their children's problems and progress (Fantuzzo, Tighe, & Childs, 2000; Jeynes, 2005).

Parents are the most significant indicator in children's development. Parental involvement influences children's achievement regardless of their cultural background and socioeconomic status. It is imperative that schools should assist the parents to understand the benefits of parental involvement in children's school readiness and preparation for kindergarten. Parents are regarded as partners with the schools in young children's development in multiple dimensions. The effects of parental involvement on young children's development have been shown to be far-reaching. Parental involvement was documented to result in improved behavior, improved attendance, and an overall high quality of education. An increasing number of people have realized that proper parental involvement was likely to help young children to develop a positive self-efficacy for school-related and community-related activities. Parental care and parental practices could have a positive effect on children's motivation, attention, assignment completion, and reduced behavior issues.

Parental involvement and school readiness

The results of Hoover-Dempsey and Sandler's studies (1997) indicated that children's school success could be influenced by their parents via four types of activities: modeling, reinforcement, encouragement, and direct instruction. For example, if parents encourage persistence in school work, their children are more likely to attain confidence and self-efficacy in their learning. Additionally, parents act as role models for education if they are actively involved in children's education-related activities. Children will tend to internalize this value and regard school as valuable(Hill & Taylor, 2004). Exposure to more education-related activities outside of school might lead children to become more familiar with school tasks and turn to be more competent performers in school (Grolnick & Slowiaczek, 1994). In spite of the fact that parental involvement has a variety of forms, Hoover-Dempsey and Sandler(1997) proposed that any form of parental involvement would affect, and to some extent predict school outcomes of children.

Numerous studies have supported the positive linkages

Chapter 2 Literature Review

between parental involvement and children outcomes, including language skills, academic skills, socio-emotional competence, positive behaviors and attitudes, and so on (Arnold, Zeljo, Doctoroff, & Ortiz, 2008; Connell & Prinz, 2002; Hill & Taylor, 2004; Li & Rao, 2000). Effective parental involvement in their children's education has been proven to predict children's success in school more strongly than family social or economic status. From the study of Schargel and Smink (2001), children with their parents' involvement in their education scored higher and had high school completion rate. Studies also reveal that there exist long-term effects of parental involvement in children's further schooling in the future. The findings of a longitudinal study, conducted by Patrikakou, Weissberg, Redding, and Walberg(2005), demonstrated a positive association between parental involvement and academic achievement for students from the 8th grade to the 12th grade. Furthermore, home-based communication between parents and children are also a strong predictor for children's cognitive development. A great deal of literature evidenced that children from families rich in books and parent-child shared reading are more likely to score higher on literacy than those from families less rich in literacy(Faires, Nichols, & Rickelman, 2000; Sénéchal & LeFevre, 2002). All these findings point to parental involvement exerting great effects on children's learning and school performance. Parent-child interaction prior to children's formal schooling facilitates school readiness and also conduces to academic success in the future schooling (Mehaffie & Fraser, 2007). Recent literature has concentrated more on how specific strategies and practices of parental involvement can promote children's school readiness. For instance, Fantuzzo, McWayne, Perry, and Childs (2004) indicated that family involvement is strongly connected to children's level of school readiness. Owing to provision of more continuity between home and school, children with parental involvement in early education transit from preschool to kindergarten smoother. Taylor and Clayton (2004) found that parental participation in activities like recognizing letters, words, reading to children, and practicing counting could better prepare children for formal schooling, but more research is needed to clarify the predictive associations between parental involvement practices and their children's school readiness outcomes.

Even though many studies indicated a positive relationship between parental involvement and children's academic and school success (Connell & Prinz, 2002; Hill & Taylor, 2004; Li & Rao, 2000; Patrikakou, Weissberg, Redding, & Walberg, 2005; Taylor & Clayton, 2004); Gilland and Reynolds (1999) argued that many studies overlooked confounding factors related to demographical characteristics. Parents' marital status, educational levels, and employment status are all found to be related to the extent to which parents are engaged in home-based, school-based, and home-school associations (Fantuzzo et al., 2000; Laforett & Mendez, 2010; Wanders et al., 2007). For instance, parents receiving higher levels of education and income have been discovered to invest more energy, time, and money in their children's early education (Guryan et al., 2008; Welsch & Zimmer, 2008). According to the study of Holloway, Yamamoto, Suzuki, and Mindnich (2008) on Japanese mothers' involvement in their children's education, it was unfolded that mothers with higher levels of education and income afforded more in supplementary lessons. On the contrary, lower levels of education and lower socio-economic status have strong association with less parental involvement (Fantuzzo et al., 2000; Kohl, Lengua, & McMahon, 2000). Transportation problems, financial problems, and inflexible working hours all hinder parental involvement. Hence, it is of great necessity to take into consideration parents' socio-demographic characteristics while examining the effects of parental involvement practices.

Parental involvement and school readiness in Chinese families in the U. S.

Chinese parents differ from their Western counterparts in traditions, value systems, and socialization goals (Chao, 2001). They are confronted with the conflicts and combinations of the two different cultural ideologies. Given Socratic influences, the United States often regards learning in a utilitarian light where knowledge is obtained primarily in order to understand the world, promote one's skills, and achieve one's goals(Li, 2005; Tweed & Lehman, 2002). Learning is viewed as engaging the gain of knowledge by means of individual attributes, including interest, abilities, and engagement(Li, 2005), which are seen to be relatively fixed(Heine et al., 2001). On the contrary, China, in which Confucian teaching is central, views learning as more than simply the pursuit of knowledge and regards learning as moral endeavor (Li, 2005). Learning consists of continual self-improvement to acquire moral ideals, such as persistence, diligence, concentration, enduring hardship, and so on. These diverse beliefs about learning are held in Chinese families in the United States.

In accordance with Baumrind, three different parenting styles existed, including authoritarian, authoritative, and permissive parenting(Baumrind, 1966). Among them, the first one was authoritarian parenting style which emphasized confrontive and coercive discipline(Baumrind, Larzelere, & Owens, 2010). Authoritarian parents were highly restrictive and demanding, relatively unresponsive to the children, and less warm.

In contrast to authoritarian parents, authoritative ones employed confrontive and non-coercive discipline(Baumrind et al., 2010), and they focused on both children's psychological autonomy and parental rules on their kids' behaviors(Wu et al., 2002). The children can attain a high degree of emotional security from their parents and they were encouraged to commit bidirectional communication for the sake of better understanding between parents and children. Additionally, parents of this type were inclined to afford guidance and expectations for their children's behaviors (Baumrind, 1966).

Permissive parenting, on the other hand, was related to a nonpunitive, accepting manner to the children. The parents were reluctant to establish restrictions to control their children's behaviors and avoid encouraging children to obey externally defined standards and rules (Baumrind, 1966). What's more, they even ignored children's unpleasant behaviors and would rather not punish children heavily when they make mistakes. Compared to authoritarian and authoritative parenting, fewer parents were defined as permissive(Milevsky, Schlechter, Netter, & Keehn, 2007).

In spite of the general findings about children outcomes linked to Baumrind's parenting styles in the realm of European American children, there existed inconsistent results in the literature regarding how well Baumrind's model of parenting styles apply to those of Chinese American families. So it appeared that the influences of diverse parenting styles on children development were far more complicated when it came to the cultural context. The positive effects of authoritative parenting style on children outcome were challenged in the minority groups, like Asian

American, Hispanic American, and African American. It has been found that mainland Chinese and Chinese immigrant parents were significantly more authoritarian and less authoritative than those in western cultures, especially U. S. and Australia(Leung, et al., 1998; Wang & Phinney, 1998). According to Chao's researches, authoritative parenting was highly associated with children's well-being and school performance among European Americans, but just mildly among the second generation Chinese Americans, and almost no linkage to the first generation Chinese Americans(Chao, 1994).

Apparently, Chinese American mothers had their specific features different from Chinese traditional mothers in that they have already attained access to western mainstream education wisdom and still been influenced by their inherited educational origins from Chinese ancestors. Compared to western mothers, mainland Chinese mothers were reported to have lower level of warmth and democratic participation for preschoolers(Wu et al., 2002) and significantly higher level of physically mandatory and verbally harsh practices(Leung et al., 1998). Additionally, the researches on Chinese mothers in Chinatown, New York City have shown that they seem to employ punishment to achieve behavioral regulation, including withdrawing their children from family social life and depriving them of privileges instead of physical punishment.

In terms of the studies of Wang and Phinney(1998),

immigrant Chinese mothers acted more authoritarian than Anglo-American ones, but their preschoolers performed better than Anglo-American children on cognitive competence. Some other studies, however, revealed that even though Chinese American and European American parents were engaged in different parenting styles, there existed no significant diversity in their young children's social competence(Jose et al., 2000). What's more, some studies found that both Chinese American and mainland Chinese parents were, to some extent, more authoritative than authoritarian when they rear their children, especially their preschoolers(Cheah, Leung, Tahseen, & Schultz, 2009; Chen, Dong, & Zhou, 1997).

Apart from Baumrind's model of parenting style, Kagitcibasi also put forward his family model of psychological interdependence which was highly associated with the coexistence of parental control, emotional relatedness, and autonomy orientation across Asian families (Kagitcibasi, 2005). A large number of studies supported the idea of this coexistence(Lin & Fu, 1990; Stewart, Bond, Deeds, & Chung, 1999). In the cultural concept in China, there is a word "guan" (control) which might have somewhat negative annotation in English. However, most of Chinese families control their children out of love(Chen & Luster, 2002).

Ideas regarding the role of parents in children's education and development differ in the two cultural ideologies. Owing to the cultural orientation toward independence in the United States (Markus & Kitayama, 1991), European American parents view cultivating a sense of autonomy as crucial in children's development (Chao, 1996). Many of them see intense academic training as inappropriate, even detrimental to young children (Hirsh-Pasek, 1991). They tend to place emphasis on the development of the whole child, not only in academic adjustment but also in emotional and social adjustment (Parmer, Harkness, & Super, 2004). Instead, Chinese parents view children's learning as a main responsibility of parents and this is reflected in the Chinese notion of *guan*, which entails meanings of "to govern" and "to love" so that young children will not fall short of standards, especially in the academic arena (Tobin, Wu, & Davidson, 1989).

The different cultural ideologies concerning children's learning and parents' role in it are likely to result in diversity in the quantity and quality of parental involvement in their children's learning. In terms of quantity of parental involvement, according to Ng, Pomerantz, & Lam (2007), European American mothers contribute less attention to helping their elementary school children with cognitive tasks compared with Chinese mothers. In terms of quality, American parents emphasize the role of autonomy in learning and accompany their involvement with dampened control and enhanced autonomy support. For instance, American parents do not insist on checking with their children's homework, allowing their

Chapter 2　Literature Review

children to decide on the parental involvement of a certain manner.

Traditionally, Chinese parents pay substantial attention to children's education and are inclined to regard children's learning as one of their primary responsibilities(Luo, Tamis-LeMonda, & Song, 2013). As a prevalent Chinese saying goes, if a son is uneducated, his father is to blame. Traditional Chinese parenting attaches more importance on parental duties of supervising children's education and emphasis of academic achievement(Chen, 1998' Ho, 1986). Most Chinese parents view children's schooling and learning as the focus of family activities, and they are willing to be involved in their children's learning and schooling.

However, Chinese parents are more willing to be engaged in home-based learning activities than those of school-based. For instance, Lau, Li, and Rao(2011) revealed that Chinese parents had more home-based involvement than school-based in their children's early education. Their findings also indicate that home-based parental involvement more strongly influences children's school readiness in a variety of domains than other types of parental involvement. From the point of view of most Chinese parents, they trust the pedagogical practices of teachers. So their interactions with teachers and their engagement in school-based activities decrease compared with their home-based involvement practices. Chinese parents tend to instruct their children in a time-structured and systematic way compared with their Western counterparts (Huntsinger, Jose, Larson, Krieg, & Shaligram, 2000). Given the differentiated practices of Chinese parental involvement, it seems important to explore the influence of Chinese parental involvement on their children's school readiness outcomes.

Theoretical Framework

Social constructivist theory of child development

Lev S. Vygotsky, born in Russia in 1860, led a group of scientists studying areas of psychology, defectology, and mental abnormality. His work remained unnoticed in the United States until the 1960s (A. R. Luria in preface to Vygotsky, 1978). His theory on social constructivism built a framework for a clear understanding of young children's development and appropriate developmental instruction. His research attached importance in a developmental approach that highlights children as active participants in their acquisition and development. At each stage of development, children are learning tools as they make sense of, understand, and interact with the environment. By means of connection with a variety of people and objects, they create their own understanding of their world. He pointed out that the growing complexity of young children's behavior is mirrored in the changed means they employ to fulfill fresh tasks and the corresponding reconstruction of the psychological processes(Vygotsky, 1978).

His theory on social constructivism built a framework for a clear understanding of young children's development and appropriate developmental instruction. His research attached importance to a developmental approach that highlights children as active participants in their acquisition and development. At each stage of development, children are learning tools as they make sense of, understand, and interact with the environment. By means of connection with a variety of people and objects, they create their own understanding of their world. He pointed out that the growing complexity of young children's behavior is mirrored in the changed means they employ to fulfill fresh tasks and the corresponding reconstruction of the psychological processes (Vygotsky, 1978). Different from Piaget, Vygotsky paid more attention to the application of theory into educational practice among school-age children.

Children's development is a process that deems education could not be delivered only in one size. Children grow at varying abilities and rates. Lev Vygotsky depicted children's visible operating level compared with potential level with guidance and support from an adult or a more capable peer as the zone of proximal development. On the basis of the notion that learning should be matched in some way to the developmental level of a child, Vygotsky put forward that we build two developmental levels. The "zone of proximal development" is viewed as the window of opportunity for an adult to approach child's experience and move the child to a higher level of thinking than what the child could achieve independently. The lower level of the zone refers to the child's ability when working alone; the upper level refers to the child's capacity when working with adult support. He defined the zone of proximal development as the length between the actual developmental level as defined by independent problem solving and the level of potential development as defined by solving problems with adult assistance or in cooperation with more capable peers(Vygotsky, 1978).

The strategy of scaffolding was made use of by the adults to question and discuss issues with the young children, which would move them into a higher level of thinking. The transition from a young child cooperating with an adult to thinking independently does not take place suddenly. It does have a gradual process. Firstly, the child works in an inter-psychological place, where the child receives an external order from an adult to take charge of impulses. Later on, more and more social experiences become internalized, self-regulated, and the command comes from within. And children's problem solving is reached with the guidance of adults who control the interaction to happen just beyond the children's abilities.

Kagan et al. (1995) supported stages of development as multi-dimensional and contextually and culturally influenced over time. Formal school readiness is, likewise, developed over time and affected by young children's own characteristics and interactions with the environment. Apart from this, Vygotsky regarded play as an essential part of young children's development. Children initiate with imaginary situations that closely mimic the real life in play. Vygotsky(1978) stated that play is an activity with purpose. Play is the tool and creature of children as they master the complicated work of growth and maturation in understanding their world.

In addition, speech development is a process that starts when a word is used to indicate something with meaning. The word is applied to express the meaning by sound. From the perspective of Vygotsky(1978), thought is not merely expressed in words; it comes into existence by words. Each thought tends to link something with something else in order to build a connection between things. There are two planes of speech, including the internal speech, and the external speech. The internal speech is the meaningful semantic aspect of speech while the external speech is the phonetic aspect. They work together to produce the unit of thought and expression.

The social constructivist theory of child development pointed to the importance of young children as active participants in the learning process. And the interactive process of development happens as children relate to others and begin the learning process through speech, play, and relationship.

There is no doubt that Vygotsky's theory has some limitations in that for the most part he suffered from tuberculosis and his experiments and writings often trailed off into unfinished thoughts. Many of his studies relied on his team of followers. Also, some of Vygotsky's work has been translated into English and published for the first time in the 1980s, leading to another limitation to his work.

Epstein's model of parental involvement

The theoretical framework of Epstein (1995) in parental involvement has a system ranging from proximal impact at home to distal impact from the community. Epstein (1995) figured out six types of involvement, including parenting, communication, participating in school activities, home learning environment, decision making, and community-related connection. Epstein's (1995, 2001) model relates families and schools and conveys various types of cooperative relationships between parents and schools.

The first type is concerned with basic parental obligations at home, like general home-related supervision and support, and provision of school supplies. This parenting typology involves affording basic life necessities like clothing, food, shelter, health care, and safety. Parents are encouraged to provide students with an environment conducive to finishing homework and maintaining academic success and educational achievement. The second one concerns home-to-school and school-to-home communication. Continuous dialogues between parents and schools provide parents with the opportunities to make decisions in relation to their children's education. The type of communication usually occurs in the form of

Chapter 2 Literature Review

open houses, report cards, conferences, and newsletters. The third type is comprised of the assistance from parents at school, including volunteering and actively participating in school activities. There may be some parent clubs, volunteer programs, and annual surveys to identify children's needs and encourage children's potential talents.

The fourth type deals with the home learning environment and issues, like spending time with children on learning activities, and offering learning materials. Parents are offered some information and ideas regarding how to help their children at home. And this would also help boost the children's development in social skills, homework, and so on. The fifth one emphasizes parents' involvement in the process of school decision-making, advocacy, and governance. The parents can be actively engaged in decision making of some important issues via Parent Teacher Organization(PTO). The sixth type focuses on parents' cooperation and exchange with community organizations. The parents can use resources and services of community organizations in order to strengthen family practices, school programs, and children development. In a word, the extent to which parents get engaged and the type of involvement they are involved in lead to differentiated outcomes regarding child development.

On the basis of Epstein's framework, the six types of involvement have been categorized into three dimensions: home-based involvement, school-based involvement, and home-school conferencing(Fantuzzo, Tighe, & Childs,

2000). Many recent researchers have extensively applied the three dimensions into examination of parental involvement in their studies(Fantuzzo, McWayne, Perry, & Childs, 2004; Wanders, Mendez, & Downer, 2007). Home-based involvement consists of a wide range of education-related activities at home, like providing rich literacy home environment, helping in coursework, and talking about school and academic expectations with their children. School-based involvement encompasses parents' assistance in classroom and actively engaging in workshops or other special events. Home-school conferencing acts as a linkage between home and school, like attending parent-teacher conferences, and interacting with teachers in terms of children's problems and progress.

Seginer(2006) connected Bronfenbrenner's ecological framework with the various types of parental involvement. Home-based involvement consists of part of the microsystem in children development. School-based involvement and parent-school conferencing constitutes part of the mesosystem. What's more, the macro socio-cultural environment functions as the macrosystem. It is considered that the macro-level cultural values and contexts have great influences on the quantity and quality of parent-child communication. Children's development includes a complex interplay within the environmental systems. Nevertheless, numerous studies have centered on the general conceptualization of parental involvement or on specific aspects of parental involvement (Jeynes, 2003).

Some other studies have concentrated on home-based involvement and school-based involvement(Pomerantz, Moorman, & Litwack, 2007). Very few have been conducted to examine parental involvement and children's school readiness outcomes. This current study is to direct to probe into Chinese parents' involvement guided by their perceptions and their children's level of school readiness.

The NEGP early childhood development dimensions

In consistence with Sprenger (2008) and the NAEYC (2009), the National Education Goals Panel(NEGP, 1995) put forward five dimensions of early developmental learning to prepare for school readiness. The NEGP regarded young children's well-being as a shared responsibility of family, educators, and society. The NEGP supported early childhood development and learning in five dimensions for school readiness and success. The five dimensions work collaboratively to ensure the connection in young children's development and learning and their later success in school and life. The updated 2005 report of the National Governor's Association (NGA) lists multiple areas but emphasizes five main domains to prepare young children and their parents ready for kindergarten, including physical well-being and motor development, social and emotional development, approaches toward learning, language development, and cognition and general knowledge.

Physical well-being and motor development

Kagan, Moore, and Bredekamp (1995) found that there existed a linkage between young children's health and performance in school. Malnutrition, as well as low birth weight, can greatly influence early childhood development and learning. It is necessary for young children to gain opportunities to develop gross motor skills by means of outdoor physical activities and fine motor skills through simple tasks, such as holding a crayon, buttoning a shirt, mastering a puzzle, and so on.

Social and emotional development

In this domain, children's earliest family social experiences laid a foundation for establishing relationships with teachers and friends. Stable family relationships help young children to attain a sense of self and well-being and become an integral part of school community upon their entry to kindergarten.

Approaches toward learning

Kagan et al. (1995) stated that children are unique and their approach to life differentiates greatly. It is significant to enable young children to learn and explore in a safe and accepting environment. Experiences help children explore aptitude for certain activities along with favors and dislikes. Young children can become interested in things of curiosity, explore independence, and develop a sense of self and self-confidence. During the learning and development process, children begin to have an understanding of who they are with a sense of belonging.

Language development

Kagan et al. (1995) highlighted the important role of language development in helping young children establish stronger connections with their world. Language is the tool that bridges between children and their world. And it helps children to express thoughts, feelings, wants, and needs. Language development functions as an important linkage to early literacy and reading skills.

Cognition and general knowledge

The fifth domain indicated by Kagan et al. (1995) refers to a full palette of incoming information and how young children acquire new information to make meaning and to use the information in their study and life. Young children are continuously learning new information and with the process moving forward they begin to make connections, comprehend relationships, and explore problem-solving skills. Acquisition of general knowledge is embodied in the practical realm of self-care and ability to toilet and dress, adaptation to change and routine, and contribution to basic chores and family interactions.

The five domains of early childhood development are intrinsically connected and dependent on each other. Inherent in this perspective is the belief that there exists no single or uniform standard for formal school readiness. The pace of development varies from child to child, so a child may not demonstrate all necessary skills in all areas. The target is to help children to gain competencies across the five domains with the understanding that all these domains are important (High/Scope Educational Research Foundation, 2006).

Chapter 3

Methodology

Chapter Two elaborated the literature review of this study, as well as its theoretical framework. Chapter Three consists of a restatement of the purpose, discussion of the appropriateness of the research method and design, the population and characteristics of sampling, data collection process, comparison of research techniques, rationale of type of collected data, validity, and reliability.

The purpose of this qualitative case study was to explore Chinese parents' perceptions of their children's school readiness and parental involvement guided by their beliefs. The findings of this study afforded information and recommendations to policymakers, teachers, and parents in better preparing children with necessary skills for kindergarten.

Research Method

Case study, one of the major qualitative approaches, was utilized to explore participants' perspectives by asking open-ended interview questions that offered actual words of participants in the study, provided multiple perspectives regarding the study topic, and supplied with a complex picture of the situation (Creswell, 2008). This qualitative case study is an approach that facilitates the exploration of a phenomenon within its context by means of various data sources. In this case, it can ensure that the issue could be explored through a variety of lenses which results in multiple facets of the phenomenon to be revealed and understood. Case study is based on a constructivist paradigm, which claims that truth is dependent on one's perspective and is relative. The paradigm recognizes the importance of the subjective human creation of meaning, but doesn't reject outright some notion of objectivity. Pluralism, not relativism, is stressed with focus on the circular dynamic tension of subject and object. Through the interviews, the participants are able to describe their opinions and this enables the researcher to better understand the participants' actions (Lather, 1992).

Research Design

A qualitative research design was applied to guide this study. In accordance with Yin (2003), a qualitative research is the use of a wide range of research and data collection methods in order to probe into participants' perceptions and practices with the phenomenon under study. Creswell (1998) defined qualitative research as:

Chapter 3 Methodology

An inquiry process of understanding based on distinct methodological traditions of inquiry that explore a social or human problem. The researcher builds a complex, holistic picture, analyzes words, reports detailed views of informants, and conducts the study in a natural setting.

Different from quantitative study, qualitative study demands the words, perceptions, thoughts, and experiences of the participants to interact and express their beliefs regarding the research topic. Yin (2003) indicated that qualitative researchers must be sensitive to how the study can be affected by the personal biographies and beliefs. For the sake of following the principle, the researcher must ensure that the study is carried out in a natural, unobtrusive setting and manner. In addition, the researcher is responsible for developing narrated stories to reflect the realities of the participants.

Qualitative research methods consist of five common designs, including case study, ethnography, grounded theory study, content analysis design, and phenomenological study. Case study provides the opportunity to focus on a particular event, situation, or program as heuristic, descriptive, or inductive. The case study method was used in this study in that it possesses characteristics that are most conducive in collecting data about participants' perceptions and experiences. Creswell(2005) articulated that researchers often use case study method when they take an interest in examining several individuals separately or in a group. Creswell(2005) also indicated that case study is sometimes called as an instrumental case given that it functions in focusing and unfolding information on a specific issue. Hence, the framework of a case study was an appropriate avenue to investigate Chinese parents' perceptions and involvement in their children's school readiness in one city of Southern Mississippi. Specifically, from the perspective of this case study, the author was able to concentrate on feelings, thoughts, and experiences of Chinese parents to encapsulate a deeper understanding of their perceptions and involvement in their children's formal school readiness.

Employing the case study method in this qualitative study was also important owing to the necessity to contextualize the phenomenon in question. Creswell(1998) stated that a case study was an exploration of a case or multiple cases by means of detailed, in-depth data gathering including many sources of information in context. When conducting a case study, it is of great importance to set the context of the case by demonstrating the physical setting aspects as well as the social or historical aspects of the case that are pertinent in understanding the research(Creswell, 1998). The current study was contextualized within the confines of Chinese parental perceptions and involvement in their children's school readiness in one southern city of the United States.

Merriam(1998) pointed out that a case study is descriptive, particularistic, and heuristic, and the final product of a case study is a thick description and explanation of a phenomenon under the study. The desired product of this study was to afford

Chapter 3 Methodology

a thick, rich description of the participants' perceptions and involvement in their children's school readiness in a southern city of the United States of America.

Merriam also stated that case studies are particularistic because the case study method highlights a particular event, situation, program, or phenomenon, and case studies have a heuristic quality in that it can induce the discovery of new meaning, enrich the reader's experience, or validate what is known. The responses from the participants were also applicable to this study in relation to Chinese parents' perceptions and involvement in their young children's school readiness in one southern city of the United States.

What is more, this study is heuristic since the author explored the strategies and practices that Chinese parents employed in preparing their children for kindergarten. With the data collected from interviews, an in-depth understanding and description of Chinese parents' perceptions and involvement regarding their children's school readiness are provided.

Adopting a case study design to get insight into parents' perceptions and involvement in school readiness provided important advantages. Aspers(2009) indicated that understanding the phenomena is usually achieved by intensive interviews. The purpose of in-depth interviews is to ask participants to describe and interpret experiences. The case study research design assisted the intent to find out in-depth perceptions and involvement of school readiness in that this type of research design has a foundation of knowledge and practice regarding daily life experiences(Aspers, 2009).

Research Questions

Through interviews with parents of Chinese young children, this research study will examine the following questions:

1. How do Chinese parents perceive their role in their children's school readiness and preparation for kindergarten?
2. What are the major factors Chinese parents consider to be effective in their children's school readiness and preparation for kindergarten?
3. What are strategies and practices that Chinese parents employ in their children's school readiness and preparation for kindergarten?
4. What are the factors that affect Chinese parents' involvement in their children's school readiness and preparation for kindergarten?

Population

The population and selection of a sample size is crucial in a qualitative study, even though there is no specific rule regarding the number of participants for interview processes

(Patton, 2002). In a case study, the number of participants varies, according to the topic of study (Ritchie et al., 2010). Multiple cases are often preferable to single cases, especially when the cases are not representative of the population where the cases are drawn and when a wide range of behaviors, experiences, situations, or outcomes is desirable.

Sampling

The data collected for this qualitative case study included sampling eight participants from Chinese families in a southern city in the United States with a population of over 8,859(U.S. Bureau of the Census, 2016). The method of research sampling depends on research questions in the study(Leedy & Ormrod, 2010) and a qualitative study normally includes small sample sizes and requires a pragmatic and flexible approach(Marshall, 1996). Qualitative sampling often applies non-probability purposive sampling rather than a random sampling approach(Ploeg, 1999).

A purposeful homogeneous sampling research method was used to select the sample for this study, which consisted of eight Chinese families in a southern city in the U.S, four of them Chinese international students and visiting scholars, and four of them Chinese immigrants to the United States of America. Purposeful sampling means that the eight familics were intentionally selected to learn about their perceptions and involvement of their children's school readiness(Creswell, 2008). Generally speaking, homogeneous sampling is when the researcher purposefully samples a group of respondents that have defining characteristics(Creswell, 2008). The specific characteristics that the present study's sample of families possesses were thefact that they were Chinese parents of children in preschool ages or in kindergarten ages whose gender and socioeconomic status varied.

The selection of participants for purposive sampling is dependent on the questions the researcher seeks to answer (Tongco, 2007). Purposive sampling belongs to the non-probability sampling method on the basis of the judgment of the researcher and the selection of samples in a specialized population(Neuman, 2006; Russell & Gregory, 2003). After deciding on the questions, the researcher can determine the defined qualities of the participants. In order to ensure the smooth operating procedures of the research, establishment of a qualitative recruitment checklist and process was necessary. The checklist identified by the Association for Qualitative Research (2011) includes the following five steps: planning and agreeing on the sample, providing research details to participating organizations, maintaining ongoing communication between researcher and organization, providing feedback to recruiters, and determining how to address issues.

In this study, the first step was planning and agreeing on the sample, which included ensuring that the research was realistic and logical, whether flexibility during the interview process was evident, whether the timeframe of the interview process was ample, and whether consent forms were in order. The second and third steps provided research details to the potential participants and maintained ongoing communication, including the letter of introduction, interview questions, and premises, and recruitment. The fourth and fifth steps provided feedback and addressed issues in the confidentiality statement and consent statement. The recruitment process for selecting the participants in this study took place by means of weekly fellowship meetings in Chinese Church and visits with four steps.

The first step of the recruitment process included attendance at weekly fellowship meetings, during which participants received a letter of introduction and got to know about the purpose of this study, the significance of the study, participant criteria, and data collection process. The participants acquired the facts that the interview included 13 open-ended questions concerning parental perceptions and involvement in children's school readiness, the interviews would be recorded to clarify or elaborate upon any comments to responses, and participants would be eligible to listen to their individual recorded answers. The author encouraged potential participants to ask questions.

After approval from IRB, the second step was to schedule an informal meeting with the selected participants to supply with an informed consent form. Participants who volunteered for this study learned about the criteria of the research study, the data collection process, and how to withdraw from this study. After participants reviewed and signed the consent form, they received the interview guidelines prior to the real interview and then decided whether to volunteer for this study or not.

In the third step, the researcher signed the confidentiality statement before the real interview. The confidential information included names, characteristics, practices, comments, or other information directly or indirectly linked to the participants. The confidentiality statement forbade discussion of any part of the study information. Research records, both electronic and hard copy, were ensured to be in a secure locked location. No suspected breach of confidentiality could occur and any suspected breach in confidentiality would have immediately spurred a report to IRB.

Step four is the interview process, in which the responses were the data used for this study purpose. Chinese parents participated in voluntary, on-site, one-time, in-person interviews lasting for approximately 60 minutes. The time commitment for this study ranged over a 3-month time span during the 2017 – 2018 school year. The interviews took place when and where it was most convenient and comfortable for participants. All the participants afforded permission for the researcher to record the interviews. The information from the interviews was transcribed by alphanumeric codes in the process of data analysis to protect the names of participants.

Data Collection

This study utilized one data collection process, interviews of the parents of young students. Ballantyne, Sanderman, and McLaughlin (2008) stated that the assessment of Dual Language Learners should include a mixture of techniques. Qualitative interviews entailed a researcher to ask open-ended questions to the participants. Open-ended questions assisted the participants to express their experiences not influenced by any perspective of the researcher or the previous research (Creswell, 2008). The researcher mainly used one type of interview, one-on-one interviews. The one-on-one interviews were conducted with eight Chinese parents, four with the higher educational background, and four receiving the lower level of education. Because the one-on-one interviews are one of the most time-consuming and costly way (Creswell, 2008), they motivated the parents to be more open and candid about their perceptions and involvement in their children's school readiness. Apart from this, interviewing one parent at a time allowed each to provide detailed information about their perceptions of preparing children for kindergarten. All the one-on-one interviews were recorded and then transcribed for analysis (Creswell, 2008). The interviews were semi-formal interviews with follow-up questions so that the parents have a chance to add some additional information regarding other themes. The first question functioned as an icebreaker for the interviewees to relax themselves and talk more(Creswell, 2008). The interview guiding questions are:

1. Could you please tell me something about your educational experience?

2. Could you please tell me some information about your children?

3. What kind of role are you in preparing your children for kindergarten?

4. What kind of education do your children receive before kindergarten, preschool or home education? Why?

5. From your point of view, will/are your children be well prepared in kindergarten?

6. What factors contributed to your children's school readiness? Why are these factors important?

7. What practices do you employ to help your children get ready for kindergarten in physical well-being and motor development?

8. What practices do you employ to help your children get ready for kindergarten in social and emotional development?

9. What practices do you employ to help your children get ready for kindergarten in approaches toward learning?

10. What practices do you employ to help your children get ready for kindergarten in language development?

11. What practices do you employ to help your children get ready for kindergarten in cognition and general knowledge?

12. Have you ever been confronted with any barriers in preparing your children ready for kindergarten in these five domains? What strategies will/do you employ in dealing with these barriers?

13. Have you ever changed your mind during the process of preparing your children for kindergarten? Why?

14. When you are engaged in your children's school readiness, what determined your strategies and practices?

15. Are these strategies and practices effective during your children's entry into kindergarten?

16. Is there anything that you would like to share with me that I did not ask?

Data Analysis

The interview data analysis process delineated by Kavale(1996) and Seidman(2006) was used by the researcher and guidance from Creswell(2008) was also sought. The data analysis for interviews is inductive since it goes "from the particular or the detailed data(e. g., transcriptions or typed notes from interviews) to the general codes and themes"(Creswell, 2008) and thus is reductionist. Creswell (2008), Kavale(1996), and Seidman(2006) commented on the interpretative nature of qualitative data analysis. Seidman(2006) stated that marking interesting passages, labeling themes, and categorizing them is analytic work in interpretation process. Creswell (2008) commented that data analysis is on the basis of the personal assessment of the data by the researcher, in view of context, feedback from participant, and the perspective of the researcher. The interpretations of the researcher may be different from those of another. The data analysis of this study included the following steps.

Step 1: preliminary exploratory analysis

Step 1 of data analysis was exploratory in nature, an iterative process initiating during data collection. Data from the interviews were collected, organized, and transcribed. Notes were referred to and portions of recordings were repeatedly listened to so that the researcher could refresh memory of content and design follow-up questions concerning areas where more information or clarification was needed. Interpretations and inferences of meanings were noted, and any personal biases were also noted. During this phase, member checks were applied to ensure the researcher fully understood what participants were trying to convey and expanded understanding of their perceptions and experiences of them.

In the management of data, transcripts were kept in a notebook and artifacts were stored in a divided folder. Electronic folders for each participant were kept with their audio files, transcripts, and other electronic data. What is more, the researcher maintained an electronic back-up of folders on an external hard drive. Documents were stored and maintained in a manner that reserved participant confidentiality.

Step 2: reduction/breakdown of text

Seidman(2006) indicates that "the first step in reducing the text is to read it and mark with brackets the passages that are interesting". The researcher must distinguish between the essential and nonessential parts on account of the study purpose and theoretical framework(Kavale, 1996). The reduction of interview data demanded both careful reading and judgment (Mostyn, 1985). The reduction of transcript data in this study was conducted by interview set. The transcript of responses from each participant's interview was read and analyzed individually and collectively. When reading each interview transcript, the researcher marked interesting passages and jotted down the codes and comments in the margins(Seidman, 2006). Creswell(2008) indicated that codes could capitalize the topics as setting and context, perspectives and thoughts of the participants, relationships, processes, strategies, and activities.

Transcripts were read without trying to locate predetermined categories (Seidman, 2006). Nevertheless, many codes representing topics of the interview questions were designed to resolve research questions, particularly when participants who could not recall information of their own were prompted. When reading a transcript continued, passages were found out to be connected to other passages.

After analyzing each participant's interview, they were contacted with if additional information was needed. Each transcript was reviewed once again to seek categories that might have been neglected from the very beginning. The coding structures across transcripts were inspected to ensure they supported the coding system and research questions. A colleague was asked to read, bracket, and code some interviews as a member check.

After all of the interviews were marked and coded, individual profiles were created, which served to reduce data further. Kavale(1996) regarded the creation of profile as "narrative structuring that entails the temporal and social organization of a text to bring out its meaning". A profile of each parent about their perceptions and involvement in their children's school readiness was created. In the profiles, the following categories were included: role, factors contributing to school readiness, parental involvement in physical well-being and motor development, parental involvement in social and emotional development, parental involvement in approaches toward learning, parental involvement in language development, parental involvement in cognition and general knowledge, and factors affecting parental involvement. These helped to analyze the data across participants and identify categories and theme.

Step 3: making thematic connections

Connections were sought across data sets when examining the interview sets and supplementary data. Deeper meaning and inferences beyond the mere words of participants were made. The researcher analyzed the data across participants to make connections and summarized similarities and differences among participants. Interpretations were conducted regarding the deeper meanings of the data when making connections across participants. When describing a tactic for making meaning, Miles and Huberman(1994) stated that noticing themes, patterns, and clustering assist the analyst in seeing what goes with what. Seidman (2006) suggested questioning what was learned while making connections.

Validity

The criteria for examining the quality of a research design were its construct validity and reliability (Yin, 2003). Construct validity could be targeted by employing multiple sources of evidence in collecting data. In this study, construct validity was attained by using triangulation. In accordance with Creswell (2003), the concurrent triangulation strategy is a method where a researcher uses multiple methods for reasons of validating data and employs findings from at least three different sources of a single study. This triangulation strategy uses multiple methods in order to neutralize the strengths of one method with the weakness of the other. In order to ensure the validity of the data collected from the one-on-one interviews, the researcher employed member checking method, in which the researcher summarized the data and then questioned the participants involved. This sharing of the findings permitted the participants to comment on and pay attention to any inaccuracies of the findings. This method was conducted at the end of each interview.

Reliability

Apart from validity, reliability is also a measure of consistency that facilitates the establishment of a study's quality. The goal of constructing reliability is for a subsequent researcher, replicating the present study by using the same procedures, to attain the same or similar results. So it means that reliability eliminates or weakens biases and mistakes in a research study (Yin, 2003). And Yin (2003) suggested using a case study protocol and establishing a case study database. Also, a peer review was adopted for validity. Score of the case study protocol should be consistent when researchers govern the instrument many times at diverse times(Creswell, 2008). When a participant responded to one question in a certain way, he should have answered a similar question in the same way.

Chapter 4

Results

The purpose of this qualitative study was to probe into the attitudes and motivations of Chinese parents and their practices to prepare children for kindergarten in a southern city of the United States. A thorough understanding of these construct can afford caregivers, parents, educators, and policy makers with insight concerning how early parenting contributes to young children's successful entry into kindergarten. Semi-formal interviews were conducted to understand the perspectives of the participants. Chapter four featured the demographic descriptions of the participants and the themes developed by means of the data analysis. Six themes emerged and descriptions of those themes with related subthemes were illustrated by excerpts drawn from the in-depth interviews.

Description of the Participants

Eight parents participated in this study and all of them

Chapter 4 Results

were volunteers who met the specific research criteria for eligibility. The data collected for this qualitative case study included sampling eight participants from Chinese families in a southern city in the United States with a population of over 8,859 (U.S. Bureau of the Census, 2016). The method of research sampling depends on research questions in the study(Leedy & Ormrod, 2010) and a qualitative study normally includes small sample sizes and requires a pragmatic and flexible approach(Marshall, 1996). Qualitative sampling often applies non-probability purposive sampling rather than a random sampling approach(Ploeg, 1999).

A purposeful homogeneous sampling research method was used to select the sample for this study, which consisted of eight Chinese families in a southern city in the U.S, four of them Chinese international students and visiting scholars and four of them Chinese immigrants to the United States of America. Purposeful sampling means that the eight families were intentionally selected to learn about their perceptions and involvement of their children's school readiness(Creswell, 2008). Generally speaking, homogeneous sampling is when the researcher purposefully samples a group of respondents that have defining characteristics(Creswell, 2008). The specific characteristics that the present study's sample of families possesses were the fact that they were Chinese parents of children in preschool ages or in kindergarten ages whose gender and socioeconomic status varied. All the participants were either the mother or father of the young child. No step-parents or guardians took part in the study. The parents were self-defined as the primary caretakers of the young children, who were the most knowledgeable about the education and care of the children. The young children primarily resided in the homes of the participants.

Seven mothers and one father took in part in this study (see Table 1). Participants reported their highest education levels. All participants had some college experience. One had bachelor's degree, four master's degrees, two doctorate candidates, one doctor's degree(see Table 2).

Belle was a 39-year-old female who had resided in the United States for eight years at the time of the current study. She got her Master's degree in business in the United States and her husband got Doctor's degree in China. Both of them work. She had only one child, a girl who was born in spring. The little girl attends a local public elementary school. Her husband moved to another state for new work. The little girl was born in the United States of America, but the family would like to set up a Chinese environment for the little girl. So they tend to communicate with the little girl in Chinese at home.

Lucy was a female who was 45 years in age and came to the United States of America as a visiting scholar for only one year. She received her Master's degree in early childhood education in China. She spent many years in pursuing her further education. So she had only one daughter born in winter who attended a local public

Chapter 4 Results

elementary school for one year. In China both Lucy and her husband work as teachers in university. But her husband lived in China during her stay in the United States. Lucy herself shed much light on English acquisition of her child back in China, so she and her child participated in a variety of activities and events held by the school, the local community, and the government.

Wing was a 39-year-old male who earned a grant to visit the United States as a scholar. He got his Master's degree in China and planned to apply for a doctorate program in the United States after he came here. Both Wing and his wife work as teachers in China. But his wife couldn't come to the United States of America together with them. He has only one boy with a fall birth date who attends a local public elementary school. The family pays much attention to the physical and mental development of the little boy, and the boy was enrolled to diverse courses both in China and America.

Angela was a 43-year-old female who had immigrated to America approximately twelve years before participating in this study. Both Angela and her husband received their Doctor's degree in America and work as researchers in a local university. They have two children, a boy studying in a local public middle school and a girl in a local public elementary school. Her daughter was born in summer and her mother tongue is English.

Daisy was a 36-year-old female who moved to America

with her husband ten years ago. They were aware that living in the United States could provide greater opportunities for her and her family. She got her Bachelor's degree in America and worked in a company. Her husband got his Doctor's degree in America and worked in the university. They have two children, a boy in a local public elementary school and a boy in a local daycare center. The older boy was born in summer. Daisy and her husband realized the utmost importance of young children's school readiness, so they made great efforts to contribute to the development of their children in various dimensions.

Anna was a 38-year-old female who immigrated to America nine years before participating in this study. Although she and her husband had earned Master's degree in China, they were enrolled in another Master program in an American university and both of them worked in the local companies. They have two children, one girl studying in a local public elementary school and a boy of only two-year-old. The girl was born in winter. The family encountered some predicaments when they tried to get involved in their children's school readiness.

Victoria was a 34-year-old female who stayed in America about three years in pursuit of her Doctor's degree. She was now a doctorate candidate while her husband graduated from a doctorate program in China. Victoria furthered her research and worked as a teacher in a Chinese university. They have only one child, a girl who was born in spring. The girl

Chapter 4 Results

spent one and a half years in an American daycare center and now she attends a local public elementary school. The family will return back to China after Victoria's graduation and they plan to take the entrance examination of a Chinese international elementary school. English fluency is also one of the evaluation criteria.

Trista was a 34-year-old female who has studied in the United States of America for two and half years. She turned to be a doctorate candidate in early childhood education program. She planned to return to China and continue her job as a teacher in the university in her mother country. Her husband worked in an international corporation in China, so he couldn't come to America for a long time. They have only one child, a girl who was born in summer. Her daughter also attended in a local public elementary school. Both parents of the family used to be athletes in China, so the kid spent much time on physical training.

Table 1 Participants' Genders

Group	F	M
Participants	7	1

Table 2 Participants' Education Levels

Highest degree earned	Bachelor's	Master's	Doctorate Candidacy	Doctor's
Participants	1	4	2	1

Table 1 and Table 2 presented the information of participants' genders and their education levels respectively.

The participants reported on basic information of their children who did not directly take part in the study. The parents afforded the age and gender of their children. Six children were female while two were male. Critical variables regarding readiness of kindergarten are gender and age (Graue, 1993a; Graue et al., 2003; Morrison et al., 1997). Children ranged in age from July 10, 2009 through August 25, 2012. Birth dates and gender characterized by quarters of the year consist of fall birth dates (September – November) 1 male; winter birth dates (December – February) 2 females; spring birth dates (March – May) 2 female; summer birth dates (June – August) 1 female, 1 male (see Table 3).

Table 3 Children's Ages and Genders

Group	Fall	Winter	Spring	Summer
F		2	2	2
M	1			1

All the participants were asked to supply with their children's total preschool experience, involving years of preschool attendance and the average hours per week the young children attended in the program. Years in preschool of the United States of America ranged from less than one year to more than three years. Three children (2 female, 1 male) received three years of preschool in the United States, one children two years of preschool in the USA, one three years of preschool in China and two months of summer camp in the United States, one three years of preschool in China and two months of preschool in the United States, two years of preschool in China and one year of preschool in the United States, and one three years of preschool in China.

Findings

Four research questions were investigated by means of the eight interviews. Face-to-face individual interviews were recorded and transcribed. The transcripts of the recorded interviews were carefully and repeatedly examined to determine the themes or common threads, within as well as across the interviews(Goodwin & Goodwin, 1996). The author read and re-read the transcripts, developing a system of coding including both descriptive and pattern codes(Miles & Huberman, 1994). Ten themes came into being, with related subthemes, during the data analysis process. Descriptions of the themes and subthemes were presented in Table 4.

Table 4 Themes and Subthemes

Themes and Related Subthemes Descriptions

Theme 1: Parents' Roles in Children's School Readiness
    1a. Guide
    1b. Helper
    1c. Fellow
    1d. Advocate

Continued

Themes and Related Subthemes Descriptions

Theme 2: Major Factors Effective in Children's School Readiness
    2a. Personality of child
    2b. Maturity, age, and gender
    2c. Peers
    2d. School-related teaching strategies
    2e. United and supportive school environment
    2f. Important family involvement

Theme 3: Parental Involvement in Children's School Readiness
    3a. Strategies and practices in physical well-being and motor development domain
    3b. Strategies and practices in social and emotional development domain
    3c. Strategies and practices in approaches toward learning domain
    3d. Strategies and practices in language development domain
    3e. Strategies and practices in cognition and general knowledge domain

Theme 4: Practices in Conquering Barriers in Children's School Readiness
    4a. Gradual adjustment
    4b. No much pressure
    4c. Encouragement
    4d. Lower expectations
    4e. Rescheduling
    4f. Rules establishment
    4g. Enrichment of parents

Theme 5: Factors that Affect Chinese Parents' Involvement
    5a. Parental perceptions
    5b. Individual characteristics of the child
    5c. Natural development of the child
    5d. Parents' peers
    5e. Family environment

Continued

Themes and Related Subthemes Descriptions

Theme 6: Suggestions Concerning Children's School Readiness
   6a. Consistent education
   6b. Natural development
   6c. Specific practices for individual child
   6d. Show and tell
   6e. Physical development
   6f. Knowledge base (literacy, spelling, and writing)

This study explored Chinese parents' perceptions and involvement guided by four research questions. It is essential to present how the themes are in linkage with the research questions in a qualitative study. The themes are tied to both the perspective and ecological framework approach of the study.

Theme 1: parents' roles

The first theme that appeared among the participants' responses was the role of parents in their children's school readiness and preparation for kindergarten. Participants reported beliefs regarding their roles as guide, helper, fellow, and advocate for their children at home, in school, and in community situations. However, some participants expressed that the practices of the preschool teachers contribute much to their children's school readiness and preparation for kindergarten. They also expressed that working with young children at home highlighted the importance of education and early readiness for kindergarten.

Theme 1a: guide

Belle believed that her role of the parent in children's preparation for kindergarten was a guide who had the responsibilities to direct young children to do the right things, such as listening to teachers in class, focusing on reading or drawing, going to bathroom independently, managing behaviors, and so on. Parents needed more patience and time for their children to become independent physically, socially, and emotionally.

> The parent is the first teacher of the child, especially young child. What the young child needs is actually what a parent [is] willing to put time and effort in ... Of course the parent is the first teacher and expected to be the best one. At that time, my daughter was just five years old and just got into the formal school environment, so mostly I guided her to do something and required her to follow some rules. Absolutely, I also tried to be a helper in many aspects in that she is a little sponge eager to absorb any information or knowledge(No. 1).

Theme 1b: helper

Wing and Victoria reported that they were helpers in their children's life and study. They refused to act like dictators in their children's life, interfering with anything and offering orders without any excuse. Instead, they tended to regard their children as active participants in acquiring information or knowledge concerning the world.

> I am a helper in my son's study and life. The teachers in preschool have huge influences on him, and I know that I have to work together as a partner. No matter he is at home or in school, he is told the same thing, and I've always exerted a real active role with his preschool teachers. Another thing is that my son is shy, so sometimes I encourage and support him to be brave or ambitious in initiating an activity, like talking with a strange child in the park (No. 3)
>
> I am a helper to my daughter and I always advocate something with no specific goals. Her entry into preschool was a good example for this. Before she went to the preschool, I read lots of stories that describe the life in the preschool. They demonstrate the differences between the home and the school and illustrate a variety of attractive activities in school. We live near the preschool and sometimes I accompanied her to experience the activities of the school and the joy to play with peer children. As a result, she anticipated the life in school. At the age of two and half, we decided to send her to the preschool, where most children hesitated to leave their parents and cried at the very beginning. But my daughter got the access to the life of preschool and she did not cry for a single time. She had a great time there with her teachers and classmates(No. 7).

Theme 1c: fellow

Lucy, Wing, and Victoria worked with their children to get ready for kindergarten. They considered themselves as fellows of their children by playing with them, learning fresh knowledge together with them, and visiting other areas of the world. They preferred to become a friend to their children and share with them about happiness and sorrow. In this way, their children were more willing to be open to them.

> I always look for books in the library and the bookstore to see whether there is any book that I can work with my daughter. We can read together with some questions answered. In addition, I also choose some little activities such as cooking and washing that also contributed to the building of those skills(No. 2).

> Eh, you know, I have always, viewed myself as fellow to him, and when he asks questions I answer them. Sometimes he is too curious and has so many questions. But I do not blow him off or tell him to ask the teacher. I try to give her correct and good answers. I have no many requirements for him and do not ask him to meet higher standards or be better than other children. I believe in a partnership with the preschool(No. 3).

> Personally I consider that any form of formal education lacks fun and interest for young children. So normally I work with my daughter at home by playing a

lot of games together with her math. She is good at her math and takes interest in doing simple things at home, not really educational. However, while she is playing she has mastered multiple skills spontaneously that are needed for kindergarten(No. 7).

Theme 1d: advocate

Angela, Daisy, and Trista believed that they acted as an advocate in their children's development and acquisition. They considered their children as inferior to them in ability to recognize the world. So they made great efforts to figure out the most appropriate activities for their children and prepare related activities for their children. They believed that their advocate of these activities was efficient for their children to be prepared for kindergarten environment.

Honestly, my contribution is so limited because my child grew up in daycare. She received education in drawing, alphabet, math, and so on. What we were mainly responsible for is the training in math, consistency with the teachers, and gradual expression of rules in school(No. 4).

We tried to provide some stimulating things at home. My son has got an iPad where he can download hundreds of apps in play-and-study. However, it was our responsibility to choose from them because many education apps contain something harmful to young children. And he also had many interactive toys that can read to him. He can go after it word by word(No. 5).

Regarding the school readiness, we have been trying to work on what my daughter missed and what she has already mastered at school. During the transition summer from preschool to kindergarten, we have determined what we need to focus on, like how to write the alphabet, how to recognize all the letters and so on. So that is something we have tried to make sure she has been ready for kindergarten(No. 8).

Theme 2: major factors effective in children's school readiness

When it came to the major factors effective in children's school readiness, all the participants mentioned specific aspects positive to their child's preparation for kindergarten. Personality of child, maturity, age, and gender, peers, school-related teaching strategies, united and supportive school environment, and important family involvement emerged repeatedly in the responses of the participants to the related questions.

Theme 2a: personality of child

Children's development was often influenced by personality of individual child. In the domains of physical well-being and motor development, social and emotional development, language development, some participants expressed that the personality of their children was a major factor in their school readiness.

Chapter 4 Results

Honestly my son is very shy, especially when he confronts the strangers. He will become silent when we have new friends at home or in the restaurant. His teachers also reported that he was at first shy and quiet in class. But many classmates volunteered to be friends with him and asked him to play with them. The teachers also spent more time with him in chatting and reading. He gradually accepted the life and study in school and played with other children more harmoniously. His talking was becoming more and more so that the teachers were pleasantly surprised at his change. He has some trouble in his social and emotional development and language development at first, but it took a favorable turn. I encouraged him instead of forcing him to talk in front of strangers(No. 3).

Probably it was because we sent him to daycare around two years old, my son interacts with his classmates, the teachers, and strangers very smoothly. He is extroverted and does not know the word "shy". He likes talking, sometimes even noisy. When we had dinner at a restaurant, he dared to talk with the children of another table about computer games. And he also likes running and playing with balls. So his development in physical well-being and motor is always above the average(No. 5).

The personality of my daughter brings both positive and negative effects in her development. Owing to the specific situation of my family, my daughter stayed in many different places, like my mother-in-law's home, my husband's brother's home, and my home. She is extremely extrovert and likes initiating conversations with other children. Articulating a short story was a task for her when she was just less than two years old. She can even argue with strangers and foreigners for some issues. She runs very fast and challenges the recreation facilities for older children. Her teachers always commented that she is so energetic. However, the negative influences of her personality came into being. For example, she refused to always listen to the orders, could not stay at the same place for a long time, and easily lost interest in learning something(No. 8).

Theme 2b: maturity, age, and gender

Cited from the responses of the participants, the readiness is also indicated by a child's maturity, age, and gender. There were common images regarding the relations between the age of children and kindergarten readiness, as well as the linkage between gender and readiness. There were some statements mentioning the inability of young boys to adapt to kindergarten environments. Several participants concerned the actual chronological age of the child as one of the markers for school readiness.

Some participants described the development and growth of their young children over time. The perception that young children have their specific pattern of development, or timetable, was reported among Chinese parents as they described gradual accumulation of skills relative to kindergarten. The word *maturity* was most often mentioned in the responses from the participants.

> We have noticed that in the last three months before kindergarten, he appeared to be organizing what he thought a little bit better, also in what he wanted and what he needed. Actually when he was four years old, we were really worried for a while because when we worked with him together for coloring pictures, it would just be a mess. It was all over the place with no order or image. Then he realized how to hold the pencil and paper in place and keep in the lines. So through his growth, we witnessed some very small things, but actually the little milestones for him(No. 5).

> I regard maturity as one of the biggest predictors of readiness, because maturity does not mean that the child reaches a high level of smartness, but it just has something to do with "Are they ready to do that? Learning the ABCs, learning the numbers, holding the pens the right way?" That is maturity in my mind(No. 1).

> You can see that there is a big difference between a 6-month-old and a one-year-old. A child of six months old can barely sit up while a one-year-old child can start walking. This is a huge difference. All the children have gone through all the development of the crawling. So I

believe that in different ages they also progress differently (No. 2).

The age of the young child and nearness to the kindergarten cut-off date of the state, that is September 1, emerged as a strong criterion for determining kindergarten readiness. Several participants mentioned the birth date as an indicator of readiness and used the birth date as a natural progressive preparation for kindergarten.

> My daughter does not have a late birthday. She has a perfect spring birthday(No. 7).
>
> As you know, young children of this state are supposed to start their study in kindergarten at five years old and so I think most people tell us, "Your child is five years old, and they can go to kindergarten now"(No. 4).
>
> Well, my son is pretty much, he has a birth date in November. So he has to go a year later than his peers. He missed it by two months. So this year, he was ready for kindergarten(No. 3).

The age-related issues were tightly linked to comparisons of children with their peers. One parent described a term "the bell curve" of age distribution, like how the abilities and ages of the children would be presented in the kindergarten cohort.

> And I want to introduce something in my son's class.

Chapter 4 Results

There were different abilities among children and the teachers did well in recognizing that and dealing with that. I know they just had to be in this bell curve and they wanted them to be right around the middle. They did not want any outliers(No. 5).

I have witnessed a lot of kids dealing with all the kindergarten readiness issues. Some parents think if their children are older they should be at the top of the class. Honestly, we all want our children to be the best. However, we expect that, but it just turned out not to be the thing. And it is the hardest thing as a parent when your children are the worst(No. 7).

Youngness was considered as especially problematic for reaching readiness. A child was generally viewed young by many participants if he or she had a summer birthday. This group of children turned five years old only a few weeks or a few days before entry into kindergarten, and in some cases, children turned five years old after kindergarten began. Youngness was considered as a red flag or warning signal of immaturity and inability to adapt to a kindergarten environment.

I found that lots of people were worried about age and some parents whose children were born in August were afraid that their children were the youngest in class. So they decided to send their children to kindergarten next year(No. 4).

On contrary to the liability of youngness, the children whose birthday dates were in fall were supposed to have an advantage both in their own maturity and when compared with their peers.

> In my opinion, in terms of age, my son stayed within his class and he was one of the older kids. So he got a few extra months in preparation for kindergarten both in school and at home(No. 3).

The statements of the participants reflected a widely agreed belief regarding school readiness that young boys tend to have more readiness issues that preclude them from smooth kindergarten matriculation. This belief was especially found among parents with both boys and girls at home. And several participants with only one child also shared the common assumption. Even though only two participants in this study had young boys, four participants commented upon age and gender. Reports regarding boys' inabilities to adapt to the structured environment of kindergarten dominated this theme.

> I can say that within only a few weeks of kindergarten you can clearly tell which child is ready. And mostly it is the young boys who should stay in preschool for one more year

probably(No. 1).

We knew it from our friends who have boys with late birthdays. They said that girls with late birthdays were likely to be more mature than boys with the same birth date periods(No. 2).

It is sort of hard for me in that I have a boy and young boys are always stereotyped as maturing and developing later than girls, especially at this age. Most people think that a girl is ready for kindergarten at the age of five, but a boy needs more training or time for preparation for some reason. I mean it is really a concept that is out there(No. 3).

Regarding that issue, I have talked to many people who I really respected and who got their degrees in education. Most of them responded like this, "you need more time to prepare him ready for kindergarten or you can hold him back for one more year because he has a summer birthday." I also talked to his preschool teachers a lot and they said that boys with summer birthday usually couldn't sit still like the other children, and maybe it took a little longer for them to attain a concept or whatever. But my son can get the concept instantly, but he still had some behavioral problems that could be directed soon because we paid much attention to his gender and birthday(No. 5).

Responses associated with boys and school readiness

concern boys' behaviors and activity levels. The statements involved the ideas that boys were disruptive to kindergarten environment and couldn't sit still in the middle of the class.

> The boy is more likely to act out if he does not get it. Behaviors like sitting there throwing pencils, playing with stuff, or doing anything else to attract attention means that he is not getting it, he is not ready. But when a girl is not getting it, she tends to sit there and become more patient. She will be more receptive to help from a friend or a teacher. A boy will always say "I can't do that; Do that for me". My son is very outgoing, very energetic, and he is a mister social butterfly. But it was a struggle for him to follow all the rules in kindergarten (No. 5).

I realize that maturity seems to be a big deal, especially with young boys. I think it is his maturity level and activity level that he is disruptive. Boys are always moving and girls are more willing to sit still in class(No. 3).

Theme 2c: peers

The influence of the participants' peers was mentioned, as their peers sometimes gave them advice on how to prepare their children ready for kindergarten and what practices should be conducted in improving their children's all-round development.

> In my opinion, every parent needs to praise their

child upon their own merits, rather than saying "Oh, now my friend is sending her child to training schools. I am afraid that they are gonna go ahead. I will also send my child to the same place"(No. 3).

Sometimes I talked about my son with my friends and they have children older than mine. But I was getting answers like "He has a summer boy, hold him back." "He is just a boy, and he has a summer birthday." At that time, I did not take their advice. But afterwards I was confronted with many behavioral problems from my son. I rethink that maybe I should send him back to preschool for one more year(No. 5).

Yes, almost everyone I met has extremely strong viewpoints. Most of my friends laid more emphasis on children's cognitive development and knowledge attainment. Some others held different perceptions. At first I raised my child naturally and she loves outdoor activities, makes friends with other children, and plays with her toys. But the practices of my friends reminded me that my daughter was over five years old and she needed to learn something. So I decided to leave her assignments on Sunday mornings, like math practices and English. Because I felt she might not be competitive compared with her peers in the future(No. 8).

Theme 2d: school-related teaching strategies and supportive school environment

Statements about school-related teaching strategies,

united and supportive school environment in the United States appeared in the responses of the participants. They thought preschool teaching contributed much to young children's preparation for kindergarten and smooth transition to kindergarten. All the participants believed that preschool provided the foundation necessary before entry into kindergarten and young children should attend preschool before kindergarten. They also expressed that kindergarten teachers noticed a vast diversity in children who had attended preschool and who hadn't.

> The preschool teacher of my daughter suggested me to send my daughter to preschool as early as possible. She mentioned that there were different levels of young children in kindergarten that came in with a significant difference in what they learned, such as letters, numbers, and sounds. Some of the children who didn't attend preschool can't even hold scissors, hold a pencil, or cut paper(No. 7).

Some parents expressed that Chinese young children went to the preschool possibly having special needs, especially the children of international students and visiting scholars. Their children haven't attained the proficiency level of English, which might hinder their communication with mates and teachers. These children with different cultural backgrounds were mixed in with a regular class of students, that is the inclusive class. The welcome and supportive school environment helped the children quickly enjoy the study and life in preschool and kindergarten.

 We had so many discussions with my daughter's teachers, both in preschool and kindergarten. They use differentiated instruction in preparing the children for the basics. Differentiated instruction, definitely, took more time to do, but my daughter's teachers found it the best method to teach young children. The school believed that the differentiated instruction would facilitate the reach to various levels of students, also beneficial to Chinese children with limited proficiency in English. My daughter learned not only some basic academic skills, but social behavior skills as well(No. 7).

 The teacher helped my daughter improve her English in many aspects, including speaking, listening, reading, and writing. They are patient when confronted with students with different cultural backgrounds, and the school has many activities that invite the parents. So we can get access to the life and study of my child. Every day there is a book in the folder of the school, which should be read and signed by me. It has cultivated the habit of reading every day for my child. She is willing to complete the reading task. But we have little time for ask & answer after reading. This is the part that I should rethink and rearrange for her(No. 2).

My child attended daycare since very young age and I have a friend who educated child at home. I have seen a significant difference in the social. My daughter has been around more children and she has a learning environment all day long. You know she was with her preschool teachers for almost ten hours a day, so there was no doubt in my mind that she was ready for kindergarten. I gave a lot of credit to her preschool teachers because they were very important for the development of my child in my mind(No. 4).

One participant stated that the different teaching strategies in American schools, compared with Chinese schools, boosted the willingness of young children to attend school. But the parent didn't mention about the reason.

Actually both the preschool and the kindergarten have some type of assessment, more informal assessment in preschool and more formal one in kindergarten. But she is not afraid of the tests. Back in China, in my generation the students were unhappy in school and worried about the results of the tests. At that time Chinese teachers were strict with students, especially in their scores. But here in America, the teachers don't place much emphasis on the results of the tests. The tests function as a check and feedback of what the students have recently learned, from which the students can find out what they are missing and try to catch up later(No.6).

Theme 2e: family involvement

Family involvement emerged frequently when it came to the factors effective in children's school readiness. Chinese parents valued the involvement in education and other aspects. They believed that proper involvement could lead to better results of their children in the future life.

> I would like to provide any possible opportunities and resources for my child. I would like to spend what I have for my child. Most of Chinese parents are even willing to sacrifice their own interest for their children. We believe that our efforts will not result in nothing. Good education is a shortcut to open the door to the labor market. Without family involvement, the children will act like a horse without rein. They will lack care, love, training, and even opportunity to receive good education. It is hard to tell their future(No.2).
>
> This might not be a good example. But our Chinese parents always do this. Whenever we met a construction worker working in hostile environment or a gasman working in severe weather, we would tell our children, "Look, if we leave you alone and don't care about your life and study, his today will become your tomorrow." I swear I will not do it again(No.8).
>
> It is my belief that parents' role modeling exerts a

great effect on children's performance. It is important to create a learning atmosphere by working together with children because it is not fair that we watch videos or do recreation activities while our children are working on their tasks alone. We also provide ample resources and materials available at home. When they are interested in dancing or soccer, the parents should supply with opportunities of learning it. In my family, there is no economic barrier in children's education and training(No. 7).

The changing era also influences the parental involvement. Before, the school had many facilities or toys that the parents couldn't afford at home. However, it is now the digital generation. We have both the traditional stuff and scientific in-depth stuff at home (No. 3).

Theme 3: parental involvement in children's school readiness

In response to questions regarding school readiness, all of the participants answered that school readiness has multiple parts and it is a mixture of different attributes and abilities. These domains corresponded to the above-mentioned five domains of school readiness identified by the NEGP(1990).

> As for me, it is everything. It is not limited to what he needs to know academically before entry into kindergarten, but it is what he is able to do when he is

required, including his social and emotional preparation, his discipline capabilities, and so on(No. 5).

There is no one specific thing about school readiness. It encompasses various aspects. It has a broad term of child's physical, social and emotional, language, academic performance, and other aspects. I think a teacher and a parent could work together to help and evaluate a child's readiness. A parent will be informed what they should focus in order to help their children. And I think it might apply more to the transition from kindergarten to first grade, but it still implies a few things(No. 7).

The domains coincided with the NEGP's(1990) descriptions of five domains of readiness: physical well-being and motor development, social and emotional development, approaches toward learning, language development, and cognitive development.

Theme 3a: strategies and practices in physical well-being and motor development

The area of physical development was mentioned by many participants. Most of the participants attached much importance to their kids' physical development. Physical readiness was closely connected with the fine motor skills needed for running, writing, and cutting in kindergarten activities.

The six types of parental involvement identified by Epstein

(1995) consist of parenting, communication, participating in school activities, home learning environment, decision making, and community-related connection. The first type is concerned with basic parental obligations at home, like general home-related supervision and support, and provision of school supplies. The second one concerns home-to-school and school-to-home communication. The third one is comprised of the assistance from parents at school, including volunteering and actively participating in school activities. The fourth one deals with the home learning environment and issues, like spending time with children on learning activities, and offering learning materials. The fifth one emphasizes parents' involvement in the process of school decision-making, advocacy, and governance. The sixth one focuses on parents' cooperation and exchange with community organizations. In a word, the extent to which parents get engaged and the type of involvement they are involved in lead to differentiated outcomes regarding child development.

The participants mentioned that they provided physical exercises guided by parents, sports equipment, nutritious meals, and nutrient supplements for their children's physical development. These belong to the first type of parental involvement.

> After she was born, we began to highlight collocation of nutrition she absorbed from the meals. She ate adequate

vegetables, fruits, and different kinds of meat. Although running is not her talent, she jumps high(No. 1).

When my daughter was very young, we purchased many sports equipment at home, like scooters of different sizes, bicycles, balls, frisbee, skipping rope, and so on. She can eat by herself at the age of two. We cook her food separately, according to a special nutritious menu. She eats more fish and shrimp than pork and chicken. We didn't allow her to throw the food she didn't like, so she is not picky in food. After enrollment in preschool, she easily caught cold because disease cross infection often took place in preschool. I worried about it for a long time, so I added nutrient supplements into her meals, including bovine colostrum powder, probiotics, zinc, and multi-vitamin. In winter and spring, I added calcium because we didn't have enough outdoor activities and sunshine. It turned out that she attended the preschool every day, not easily getting sick(No. 2).

Health is the utmost thing I care about. So I often take him out for running or playing balls. I only bought gummy bears, no other nutrient supplements. Both vegetables and meats are important for kids' development, but he is a picky eater. So I have to spend more time in cooking more colorful and delicious food for him(No. 3).

I don't require my son to eat particular foods, but he is crazy about milk. He regards it as water. Can you imagine that he can consume two gallon milk in only one week?

When he took the plane, he drank milk instead of meals. Occasionally he eats gummy bears(No. 5).

My daughter liked eating when she was a baby, so I used her favorite food to help her exercise actions like lifting and feeding. She can flexibly knead the plasticine into many shapes. I added nutrient supplements according to her special needs in each stage. I added calcium when she lost her teeth. She drinks milk and multi-vitamin every day. She eats vegetables, fruits, and meats(No. 7).

The participants didn't mention any practices of the second and third types of parental involvement. Nevertheless, one participant reported that providing an environment for exercise was important for young children to have a habit of exercise.

> We have sports equipment at home, we also organized many games in no need of equipment. She could swing by our arms, climb the body mountain, and drill the body cave. And it is now a habit for every member in our family. We are used to building up our bodies for an hour per day. We do it with her, rather than leaving her alone(No. 2).

In reaction to the change of rules in school, one participant expressed that she positively cooperated with the school and made great efforts with adaptation to the new rule.

> Transition from the preschool to the kindergarten, the timetable and afternoon nap were big problems for my kid. She had been used to the schedule of the preschool. Without the afternoon nap, she felt tired in the afternoon and couldn't handle the tasks in the afterschool program. But we had to follow the new schedule of the kindergarten, at least two to three weeks for us to work on it. Before the kindergarten started, we deliberately canceled the nap time. And we persuaded her to go to bed earlier and get up earlier too. It was a hard period for both the kid and us, but fortunately we conquered it(No. 1).

Many participants indicated that the neighboring community provided a lot of resources and activities so that they can make use of them in their children's physical development. When some organizations promoted their extra-curricular programs, many parents actively got more information and suggested their children to attend some programs according to their willingness and interest.

> The neighboring playground is a good place for kids of different ages. We play various equipment in the playground for more than one hour per day. I always encourage her to challenge equipment for older children, and when she succeeded she attained a sense of satisfaction

and self-esteem. When we are back we will miss the playground so much(No. 2).

I think more sports activities do benefit kids' physical development. So I interacted with the community organizations and sent him to some extra-curricular programs, including basketball, dancing, and drawing. He was found to have more flexible bodies than other children. So the teacher suggested that he be sent to the gymnastic program. He had fun in these programs(No. 3).

My son had little problem in physical development because both the daycare and the family paid much attention to the outdoor activities. He had at least three hours' outside every day. We also sent him to the summer camp organized by the Church. When he was four, he was interested in karate, so we sent him to karate program. But he gave up a little bit older. From then on, he regularly attended swimming class, four times per week. Our community has YMCA, which contains a lot of places for sports, like indoor swimming pool all the year. It is convenient for my son to keep swimming, not just restricted to summer. In addition, he also took part in so many afterschool activities, like soccer and baseball. But the thing is he couldn't keep on it(No. 5).

The neighboring community provided many accessible programs for children of different ages. My daughter attended many interest classes, like gymnastics, swimming, and dancing. But she didn't like them and quit quickly. Now she is enthusiastic about soccer, and soccer takes a very important part in her life. The playground is also beneficial to her physical development. She often plays with her mates in the playground, challenging recreational equipment(No. 6).

My daughter played in the community playground for more than one year, and I witnessed her change in physical development. At first she ran not very fast, compared with her American peers. But after one year, she got familiar with all the equipment in the playground and ran like the wind blows(No. 7).

Theme 3b: strategies and practices in social and emotional development domain

Being prepared socially and emotionally ready for kindergarten environment was one of the most strongly associated factors in school readiness, as all the participants mentioned their involvement in social skills in various degrees of importance. Social skills were considered by the participants as a foundation for the abilities to acquire and take advantage of kindergarten structure and curricular. Social and emotional domain of school readiness consisted of ability to separate from parents, interact with adults and peers successfully, independence, and emotional stability. Parental practices of different aspects emerged in the participants' responses, including companionship, encouragement, not too much attention, diverse family members, messages, parent-teacher conferences, volunteering, preparation for items for parties, attending parties, play dates, family dates, playmate, playground, early entry into preschool, a variety of extracurricular classes, and visits to libraries, bookstores, and museums.

Many participants expressed their practices in the home-based dimension, including encouragement, companionship, not too much attention, and diverse family members.

> My child was shy when she was very young and she didn't dare to talk with anyone not familiar to her. We were afraid at first that she couldn't fit in life in school. So we encouraged her a lot when encountering strangers and told her it was not a big deal to invite a stranger child to the home. Whenever she met a child she would like to play with, we would be supportive with her decision (No.1).

> Encouragement for children was so important that we often encouraged her to play with any child in her class or in our community. But sometimes she refused to do so and we respected it(No.2).

> My son was shy and he often refused to talk with others. So I spent much time in playing with him. And I was reluctant to force him to talk. Emm... encouragement maybe(No.3).

> I think too much attention on children also exerts negative effects on their development. My daughter

Chapter 4　Results

could not stand my attention on others' things, even for a while. For example, she always interrupted my conversation with my friends just because I didn't notice her needs of snack. So I tried not to put too much attention on her. She has to learn independence(No. 3).

My daughter had some problems with her independence and separation from parents when she was four and a half years old. At that time my son was born, and my attention was mostly paid to him after my mom left America. She refused to grow up and become independent. Crying all day in the daycare often occurred. Her teacher reported that she missed her mom a lot and didn't want to leave mom. So I promised to pick her up earlier and accompany her with her homework. And I began to balance my attention to her and her brother(No. 6).

It was hard to define my child's personality. But fear to face with strangers was one of the problems for her. So I encouraged her to make friends with unknown kids in the playground. It turned out that she had a great time with her new friends even though she was nervous with her first step(No. 7).

My daughter was extrovert and willing to communicate with others. It might be the environment and diverse family members that contributed to the establishment of her personality. She moved a lot when she was young and lived with her parents, grandparents, and uncle's family. Interaction was not a problem for her. But my frequent absence in her life resulted in her emotional instability. She couldn't accept any form of negative remarks(No. 8).

In the dimension of the second type of parental involvement, messages and parent-teacher conferences were mentioned frequently by the participants.

> In order to get familiar with the communication of my child with classmates and the teachers, I often put messages in her folder. From the teachers' replies, I could know some specific problems of my child. And the attending of parent-teacher conferences was another effective tool for me to interact with the teachers. They could inform me her progress and problems in detail so that I could take action to correct or encourage her(No. 1).
>
> Active communication with the teachers was the most efficient approach for us to get access to his life in school. The teachers tried to open his heart and close their gap. They attained my son's trust and he began to share with them about his things(No. 3).
>
> Through the regular parent-teacher conferences, we got to interact with the teachers about my child's performance and barriers in school. We found that she was open to the teachers and shared with them the interest that we didn't know. She would like to talk with her teachers about dinosaurs and history. We were glad that she was not shy in school and communicated with peers and adults well(No. 6).

Chapter 4 Results

The thing changed from preschool to kindergarten. When she was in the preschool, her teacher and principal always greeted children and we had a lot of conversations concerning my child's development. I fully understood her situation in school via messages, parent-teacher conferences, and activities. However, after her entry into kindergarten, I seldom met her teachers, so I left messages and talked with the teachers in the conferences (No. 7).

When it came to the third type of parental involvement, volunteering, preparation for items for parties, and attending parties were the expressions appearing in the answers of the participants.

When the school held parties, I would do some volunteering work. Even if I wasn't free to complete volunteering work, I would try to prepare items for parties and appear in the parties so that my daughter could be inspired and earn a sense of self-esteem. Though sometimes we were so tired, we had to ... (No. 1).

Participating a variety of activities in school was so interesting for the parents. For one thing, the children hoped that their parents could attend them and know more about children's life in school. For another thing, it was great for the parents to observe what actually happened to their children in the activities. They could precisely tell pros and cons of the activities for their children(No. 7).

No participant clearly mentioned their practices in the fourth and fifth types of parental involvement. Children were not brought up in a vacuum environment, and all the participants employed the organizations and resources in the community to facilitate their children's social and emotional development. They referred to play dates, family dates, playmate, playground, early entry into preschool, a variety of extracurricular classes, and visits to libraries, bookstores, and museums.

> Playmates of the same age were important for my kid to become open. She had many potential friends when she was young. But she was too shy to play with them. So I arranged many play dates with these children and their parents in our home or theirs. Their relationship became closer and she talked more with them(No. 1).

> To be honest, we were very selective to hang out with other families. Generally, we made friends with the parents whose children my daughter would like to play with. I was interested in organizing many activities for the families together, like birthday parties, circus show, scientific experiment, and exchange of arts and crafts. You know, when we left Shanghai for America, I knew that her friends would buy her gifts, but we didn't

want them to spend too much money. So I organized a farewell party in the drawing class, in which all the children were required to draw a card and write words on it for my daughter. No expensive gifts were accepted. It was an extraordinary activity(No. 2).

We invited some of his playmates to the home. And we sent him to arts, gym, and dancing classes, where he could meet more peers and adults. In this case, he could interact with strangers more often and become more open. In our community there is a big playground, and children of different ages come regularly to practice various equipment. It was a great tool for my son to greet more children with different cultural backgrounds. They played together and made friends with each other(No. 3).

The people I was grateful to were × × × and her mother. She was my daughter's friend and we lived in the same community. When my daughter entered the kindergarten, I was worried that her emotional instability would hinder her adaptation to a kindergarten environment. I worked until five p. m. , so × × × 's mother would help me pick up my daughter, and she had a playmate. Most of the social problems were solved because she didn't have a sense of solitude(No. 6).

Around the age of one, my daughter attended a training program for young children. She played with other young kids there and actively took part in the activities. After two years old, she was sent to daycare.

Of course she was not willing to stay at the daycare, but she found that there were many children of her age there. They could sing songs, dance, and listen to stories in class. She never expressed her dislike to daycare. I think it might be her early entry that exerted positive effects on her easy adaptation to new environment(No. 8).

Theme 3c: strategies and practices in approaches toward learning domain

The ability to fit in the kindergarten environment with a motivation to learn, curiosity, enthusiasm, and a willingness to work with school routines and structure belonged to the approaches to learning domain (NEGP, 1990). Attitudes of ready young children involved focus, enthusiasm, and curiosity. Behaviors linked to readiness involved the ability to pay attention, share, sit still, and wait. Parents trained their children in attitudes and behaviors in school and learning in order to get ready for a kindergarten environment, including encouragement, check of folder, reading, books, art crafts, bed stories, homework, community resources, and preschool. These practices belonged to the first and sixth types of parental involvement.

> She was still young in kindergarten, so I was worried about her behaviors in school. The folder informed me most of her performance in school, and I kept on checking her folder every day to see what she was

missing or what her misbehavior was(No. 1).

She was just eager to know new things, and do new things from a very young age. So I encouraged her to keep the enthusiasm and tried to provide answers to her curiosity(No. 2).

My son had a habit of reading, which cultivated his focus and listening to orders. In addition, I often took him and his playmates to the library and the children museum, where they could experience the combination of play and scientific knowledge. They were curious about some magic phenomena and were instilled with a curiosity to learn (No. 3).

My daughter was good at learning and following the directions because we trained her after she was born. For example, we spent much time with her in making art crafts and told her to follow the order step by step. She was willing to do it and did it perfectly(No. 4).

I was shocked by my son's performance in school. He never got smiles from the teachers, always the numbers to identify his behavioral problems in school. I assumed that it was partly our fault because we paid too much attention to the natural development of the child. Education of disciplines was almost absent. I regretted a lot about it(No. 5).

I think my child had the discipline to listen and she was able to follow and understand instructions. I checked her homework every day so that she knew that it was her responsibility to accept the situation and commit to instruction and respect(No.6).

In my opinion, it was more a willingness to learn or an enthusiasm about it, rather than the exact knowledge. The young children definitely need to own the ability to sit still, even just for a short period of time. My child had the motivation to sit down for a while, keep her hands to herself, and have social ability to work with a variety of kids without talking "Everything is mine". I trained her to take part in multiple games in which she and her playmates sang, danced, and played while acquiring information of the whole world(No.7).

I am an old-fashioned parent, and I only tried the old style, guaranteeing my child's homework and working with her. Initially I had a tough time with my father, neglecting her development. But my friends' actions upon their children's academic performance reminded me that I should take immediate action before her entry into kindergarten. The homework mainly covered the training of math and English, no tasks about Chinese characters. She couldn't sit down for a long time to do her homework, so I created a reward plan for her. If she completed her tasks she could get thirty stars. When she accumulated one hundred stars, she could have a gift for it(No.8).

Theme 3d: strategies and practices in language development domain

General language use and command of verbal skills was mentioned by many participants regarding its importance in school readiness. They linked language development with the ability to interact with peers and teachers about important information and needs in a busy kindergarten setting. Parental strategies and practices mentioned by the participants included reading, communication with teachers, school activities, the implementation of reading plan, picture storybooks, e-products, Chinese environment, library, Chinese class, and English class.

With regard to the first type of parental involvement, seven participants regarded reading as the most important approach to boost young children's language development.

> Reading is something that I started from the very beginning. When she was less than one year old, I read for her as bedtime stories every day. Gradually I left one or two words to her in one sentence. At first the words were very easy for her in order to establish her confidence. Then she could read more complicated words, sentences, and even paragraphs. Now I read less and less while her reading became more and more. Actually her listening developed very fast at first, and then she enriched her oral expressions. Reading is of great value to children's language development(No. 1).

I had a plan for her to read for thirty minutes every day. At first it was my job to read to her, and now it was hers to read to me. I tried to talk with her in English at home, but my limited vocabulary hindered my engagement in this part(No. 2).

Reading habit was cultivated from her birth. Honestly, my English is no better than her, so I didn't do much in her English acquisition. The preschool teachers and her peers were responsible for her English development. But we read some Chinese books to her, but she was not willing to speak in Chinese. Her Chinese acquisition was far away from fluency, especially in reading(No. 4).

My son likes reading, both in English and Chinese. He speaks English and Chinese well. We read to him at the very young age, and he was accustomed to reading books, more novels(No. 5).

Bedtime stories played a great role in her language acquisition. She could speak fluently when she was only two years old(No. 6).

My daughter was eager to listen to my reading to her when she was little. She was interested in the plot of the story and she gradually could copy the expressions in the stories(No. 7).

I intervened with her language development when my daughter was only six months old. I read stories in the picture books to her, and she was interested in the colorful pictures at first, and then the stories themselves. She could tell a story at three years old(No. 8).

In relation to the second and third types of parental involvement, many participants highlighted communication with teachers, school activities, and implementation of reading plan, which facilitated their cooperation between the school and the parents.

> The teacher had a reading plan for each child, which provided important opportunities for them to keep reading. What I did was to work with the teacher and help my child to complete the daily reading task. Sometimes I emailed to the teachers in order to get more information about her progress and problems. The teachers replied elaborately and invited me to take part in a variety of activities so that I could closely observe my child for her language development and her communication with peers and teachers(No. 2).
>
> Owing to my son's cultural background and his introvert personality, I didn't expect that he made noticeable progress in a limited time. I interacted with the teachers by means of social apps and tried to participate in all the school activities even though sometimes my work in the university occupied most of my time. For example, recently the school held a Halloween fair mainly regarding American Indian Tribe.

> We actively contributed to the preparation of clothes, food, and drums while the teachers decorated the clothes, made accessories, and did the face-painting. While enjoying their performance, we also got the clue about their language development and social development in school(No. 3).
>
> We worried about her Chinese development rather than her English acquisition. We interacted with the preschool teachers about her language, and they agreed upon our decision to provide a Chinese environment at home(No. 4).
>
> Her mother tongue developed very smoothly in China, so I didn't worry about her language development at first. But after she was enrolled in preschool, she refused to talk to both children and teachers in English. I communicated with the teachers a lot about this, and they expressed their attention to her English development(No. 7).

No participant shed light on the fourth type of parental involvement, but they practiced much and expected more in the fifth and sixth types of parental involvement, including picture storybooks, e-products, Chinese environment, playmates, library, Chinese class, and English class.

> At first I tried to supply with an English environment at home, like speaking in English and sticking English words on items. But it was hard for me to keep speaking English. In

Chapter 4 Results

addition, I transacted a library card and regularly borrowed thirty books which we read in three weeks. The library functioned as a major resource for my daughter and me to learn English. We could watch DVDs in the library. At home I bought an iPad for her so that she could download multiple applications beneficial to her English development. However, the harm to the eyesight from the e-products couldn't be neglected, so I am looking for a better way to decrease the negative effects (No. 2).

When my son was in China, one of my friends recommended an English native speaker to be the teacher for five to six children. And it was said that second language learning should be initiated from a young age. So we sent him to the small-size class, where the children could communicate with the foreign teacher while playing. After the class, we designed an English class at home and he acted as a teacher to tell us what he learned. He favored the game and was enthusiastic about being a leader or a teacher of us. In addition, we bought many picture storybooks from bookstores and borrowed DVDs and books from the library. Because the recent version of laptops had no DVD players, I bought a DVD player from BestBuy so that he could enjoy the movies and videos at home and get more English expressions from them(No. 3).

We bought many Chinese books from Taobao or

bookstores from China. We speak Chinese at home till now. But her first language is English and she is in favor of English storybooks more(No. 4).

We provided a Chinese environment at home and my son liked reading Chinese books. He has no accent when speaking in Chinese. He had Chinese class in church(No. 5).

We didn't speak English at home, but she only knew some simple Chinese expressions at first. She didn't get rid of the accent in oral Chinese until she played with her Chinese friends. When they played together and had more communication, their speaking in both Chinese and English made great progress. After we moved to another community, she had no many Chinese playmates, so we sent her to Chinese class in church. Now she could write some simple words(No. 6).

Compared with the reading list from the teacher, my daughter was more interested in the books from the library. She found that the stories were funny and fresh (No. 7).

I borrowed picture storybooks from the library and read to her as bedtime stories(No. 8).

Theme 3e: strategies and practices in cognition and general knowledge domain

In this domain, the readiness consisted of acquisition of specific cognitive abilities as well as a general knowledge base. The skills ranged from a basic set of knowledge like shapes, colors, numbers, and letters, to life skills like knowing address, full name, and phone number. The participants mainly focused on their children's math skills, writing, and general knowledge base. They were involved in their children's development by means of the following practices, including questions & answers, reading, math games, math training, and math in daily life. Generally speaking, these belonged to the first and fifth types of parental involvement.

  Young children are very curious about the world, so they always asked many questions, to which I tried to give answers. And sometimes I asked her questions to enhance her understanding of general knowledge. She did well in math in school. It might be partly because we trained her in our daily life, like numbering when climbing the stairs(No.1).

  I think reading could solve all the problems, including increasing her knowledge base. She could know about geography, science, culture, and history through reading books. And she liked math games with me. For example, we recorded the points when brushing teeth. She knew the numbers and tried to have more numbers than me. In our daily life, we had so many activities to train her math, like climbing the stairs and jumping ropes(No.2).

  I didn't pay much attention to his acquisition of

cognition and general knowledge, so he was short of a general knowledge base. But I replied to his many whys(No. 3).

Compared with children of other races, Chinese children received more training in math and general knowledge. That might be the major reason why they had better performance in math in school(No. 4).

The parents have to answer the questions of the children, no matter how many the questions are and how weird the questions are. They are in the process of acquisition while getting the replies. We conducted math training in our daily life. And after we witnessed that Chinese parents whose children received education in China assigned many math training homework, we also required her to practice arithmetic after class. She had a solid foundation for her future study in math and science (No. 6).

When my daughter was very young, we had many math games, like numbering the apples that she ate and counting money in both Chinese and English(No. 7).

Homework in math helped her to practice numbers and logical thinking(No. 8).

Theme 4: practices in conquering barriers in children's school readiness

When the participants referred to the practices they employed to eliminate or alleviate the barriers in their children's preparation for kindergarten, gradual adjustment, no much pressure, encouragement, lower expectations, rescheduling, rules establishment, and enrichment of parents frequently emerged in their replies.

Theme 4a: gradual adjustment

Belle reported that the gradual adjustment was the practice that she applied when confronted with any barrier in her daughter's development. She tried to respect her child's individual characteristics and treated the development as a gradual adaptation process.

> The changed timetable was a big problem for my child, so we planned a new timetable for getting up and going to bed. At first she couldn't follow the new timetable and was late for school for a few times. We didn't blame her; instead, we afforded a period of time for her to gradually adjust to the kindergarten environment. She got used to it and loved the kindergarten life now(No. 1).

Theme 4b: no much pressure

Lucy, Anna, and Victoria reported that they found that the efficient way to alleviate the negative attitudes of children was not to lay much pressure to children. Young children were not mature and they often could not control their desire to disobey orders. So no much pressure would ease their relationship with the parents.

In the study of English, she felt a little bit frustrated because she was too shy to talk to her classmates. I encouraged her to talk regardless of accuracy in expressions. I also made great efforts not to lay much pressure on her(No. 2).

In general, my child had a natural development process with no much pressure from us. She had no overburden in homework(No. 6).

Her refusal to talk in preschool almost drove me crazy. I knew that she had the ability to communicate with her peers and parents, but she kept silent in preschool. Her teacher sent me messages to report her talking. When she talked one time in preschool, all the classmates and teachers applauded for her. The first day of her entry into kindergarten, I just told her teacher that she was not new here in America and she could speak English. Surprisingly, she communicated with her kindergarten peers smoothly. So I think too much attention to the child might not be a good thing and children may easily get allergic to the attention. It is better to develop language in a natural environment(No. 7).

Theme 4c: encouragement

All the participants mentioned that they encouraged their children to communicate with peers and teachers, learn skills in school and at home, and participate in outside activities. Encouragement, not pressure, played a critical role in their establishment of confidence and self-esteem.

> She was encouraged to talk with native speakers even though she only knew some simple words. But she did it successfully(No. 1).
>
> My son is a shy boy. He dared not to ask his teachers for help. So I encouraged him to say thanks to strangers, shake hands with my friends, and have play dates with other children(No. 3).

Theme 4d: lower expectations

Wing indicated that the reason of the parents' frustration came from their high expectations. So it was lower expectations that could stop parents' anger towards their children's performances.

> To be honest, we were sometimes disappointed by our children's performance. It was the high expectation that strained the relationship between parents and children. Lowering your expectations might be an accessible way for parents to guide the children(No. 3).

Theme 4e: rescheduling

Lucy reported that another practice that she employed in eliminating the barriers of her daughter's language development was rescheduling. The efforts of parents had bigger influences on children's development in multiple domains. It was the parents' obligation to guide their children and manage their children's behaviors.

> Another big barrier we met was that we couldn't have enough time for story reading and ask & answer. So I rescheduled the timetable for dinner, thirty minutes earlier than before. In this way, we had thirty minutes for reading and ask & answer(No. 2).

Theme 4f: rules establishment

Anna expressed the uncontrolled anger when her daughter was rude or refused to complete tasks. The children were so smart that they could observe their parents and adjusted their strategies accordingly. So a harsh attitude was a necessity in establishing rules.

> But there were some occasions when she misbehaved beyond the gauge of my tolerance. Harsh attitude of rule establishment was needed(No. 6).

Theme 4g: enrichment of parents

Lucy and Trista reflected upon their strategies and practices, and they found that enrichment of themselves were also primary in dealing with some barriers of their children's preparation for kindergarten. The lack of knowledge base, fluency in English, and patience hindered their involvement in their children's school readiness.

After communicating with the teachers, I found that my inadequacy in English resulted in my inability to help my child. So my daughter and I studied together and enriching myself was the first task(No. 2).

My thoughts couldn't parallel my actions. My career was a big barrier in my child's preparation for kindergarten. And I was the first to be a parent. There is too much that I need to learn. Enriching myself is the first task for me(No. 8).

Theme 5: factors that affect Chinese parents' involvement

Statements about the factor that affect Chinese parents' involvement were present in most of the interviews, in which participants believed that parental involvement in children's development was crucial and the factors that affected it included parental perceptions, individual characteristics of the child, natural development of the child, parents' peers, family environment.

Theme 5a: parental perceptions

Most of the participants indicated that Chinese parental perceptions were highly positively related with their activities. This was consistent with Chinese dominant philosophical principles that various viewpoints of the world result in various behaviors.

It depends... Most Chinese parents are subjective

when they decide on their practices. What they believe is one of the most important elements in educating children. Maybe I am among them. Some parents lay much emphasis on what they think is important. For example, some parents had a dream to become a famous pianist, but they couldn't realize it. So they decided to copy the same dream in their children(No. 8).

My perceptions decided my activities. From my perspective, young children should attain new experience and acquire new knowledge as much as possible. But I also think that anything related to education will discourage children's interest in it. So I played a lot of games together with her. She was happy to learn something in the games. If she was unwilling to take part in the games, I never forced her to complete them. What I believe is that adults need to spend much time in educating children, but they ought to spread knowledge or share experience with no trace. And the children could be unconsciously influenced(No. 7).

My wish for my son is that he will grow up healthily and happily, with some specialties. His life in the future will not be only restricted to his academic performance. I hope his life will be rich and colorful in many aspects. What I believe guided what I do(No. 3).

Theme 5b: individual characteristics of the child

Lucy, Anna, Victoria, and Trista described that they

Chapter 4 Results

determined their parental practices and strategies according to the individual characteristics of the child. They reported that the successful model of a certain child might not be applied to their own child, and they conducted specific practices appropriate to their own child.

> As a parent, what I have to understand at first is the stages of development for each child. I need to prepare beforehand for what my child needs in each stage and what is the most efficient way to guide my child(No. 2).
>
> My engagement depended on the development of my child and the possible ways that I can do to help her. I thought my child had some problems with communicating with strangers, so I involved more in this aspect, like encouraging her to take part in more activities and providing more opportunities to meet people of all forms. Gradually she became more comfortable when encountering strangers (No. 6).
>
> Before I decided upon my activities, I spent much time in observing her and found out her characteristics and her favors. Afterwards, I adopted a positive attitude and arranged many activities to stimulate her potentials(No. 7).
>
> The emphasis should be placed differently owing to the characteristics of individual children and family environment. Each child is distinctive with unique skills and gifts(No. 8).

Theme 5c: natural development of the child

Victoria and Trista mentioned that they attached much importance to the natural development of the child, so they hesitated to push their children to do any additional exercise out of their reach. The children were treated in a more natural and harmonious environment.

> I believe that young children were born with love of learning and acquiring. I never discouraged her or set up many strict disciplines for her(No. 7).
>
> Some children need more attention regarding their social and emotional development while some other children require more attention to their language development. So what the parents should engage in their children's development mainly depends on the differing degrees of development in each domain. The observation of parents and close communication with teachers place an important part in catching sight of that(No. 8).

Theme 5d: parents' peers

Five participants had no experience in educating children because they had only one child at home. Their peers sometimes gave them advice on how to prepare their children ready for kindergarten and what practices should be conducted in improving their children's all-round development. Their parental involvement was partly influenced by the suggestions from their peers.

Chapter 4 Results

We had some gatherings with parents in the same community, and they often provided with valuable suggestions regarding how to educate children and boost their development. However, some of them were effective for my child while some others not(No. 1).

I was busy with my second child when my daughter attended kindergarten. My friend and her daughter helped me a lot by spending most of the time with my daughter. She observed her behaviors and advised me to care much about her in certain areas. I owed her a lot(No. 6).

Theme 5e: family environment

Parents played a great role in young children's development of various domains. A supportive and harmonious family environment was of great significance to the development of the children. Lucy and Victoria highlighted the importance of family environment and its effects on parental involvement.

I have multiple plans in systematic preparation of approaches and perceptions. However, I can't realize all of them owing to lack of time, individual parental styles, insufficiency of execution abilities, and family environment. For example, my husband and I work in different cities and mostly he takes care of my daughter while I work in another city. So the cooperation can't work that smoothly sometimes. I wished I could spend more with my child in practicing the piano more, but I was not able to quit my job, the earning of which also supported my family. To do or not to do is a hard problem(No. 2).

The environment in my family is supportive and warm(No. 7).

Theme 6: suggestions concerning children's school readiness

A few participants admitted their inadequate involvement in their children's preparation for kindergarten. And a few realized what they missed after their children's transition to kindergarten. When it came to the suggestions about children's school readiness, the participants mentioned consistent education, natural development, specific practices for individual child, show and tell, physical development, and knowledge base (literacy, spelling, and writing).

Theme 6a: consistent education

Victoria strongly regretted her leaving her daughter with her parents for half a year. The young girl could not tell which policy she should obey. No consistent education was harmful to the children's development. They got confused about what was wrong and what was right. Also they easily found out the practices to make their parents yield to them.

My daughter experienced two different types of

Chapter 4 Results

education owing to my first year's study in the United States. The inconsistent education confused her and she felt unsafe in unfamiliar circumstances. She tended to occupy me for a whole day and threatened me if she couldn't reach her target. So I strongly suggested that there should be consistent education within a family(No.7).

Theme 6b: natural development

Anna regarded her as a friend of her daughter and she respected her natural development. The different developmental stages of the children marked in the changes of children in their behaviors and acquisition of information and knowledge.

> Although we are the parents, we have to respect the children's natural development(No.6).

Theme 6c: specific practices for individual child

Both Trista and her husband were professional sportspersons, so their child was very energetic and active from her infancy. They could not treat their children as a normal child. Instead, they employed specific practices for their child, such as more exercise hours daily for her, more outdoor activities, trainings in her running and jumping skills, and so on.

> I could say there was no universal textbook for

parental strategies and practices. Different children had different characteristics, which required different practices (No. 8).

Theme 6d: show and tell

After her son attended daycare center, Daisy participated in multiple activities in school and observed that a variety of teaching strategies could boost the children's confidence and self-esteem. They could easily articulate about their own opinions and defend themselves. Among them, show and tell helped the children acquire skills of public speech. The parents could make use of this activity at home to practice their children's language.

And they also could make use of show and tell to practice their children's ability in public speech and debate(No. 5).

Theme 6e: physical development

Belle believed that parents should emphasize the physical development of their children owing to the longtime stay in school during the day. Many children in the United States had to stay at school for ten hours, so the parents should make sure they had enough energy to handle all the activities in school. Physical development of the children was the priority to most parents.

My daughter also attended the afterschool program frontier, so she needed to stay at school for ten hours. That was a challenge to her energy. So it was crucial for the parents to get engaged in their children's physical development, such as nutritious meals, enough exercise, and so on(No.1).

Theme 6f: knowledge base (literacy, spelling, and writing)

Lucy, Wing, and Daisy reported that apart from children's physical development, their acquisition of knowledge base was also primary in children's preparation for kindergarten. They received lessons from their own children. The neglecting of the knowledge base would result in many barriers of children's future academic career.

 I used to shed light on children's play and physical development, no emphasis on their preparation for knowledge acquisition. But after my child entered kindergarten, I realized that the emergent literacy was necessary for children to better adjust to the study in kindergarten. So I suggested that parents should prepare their children for emergent literacy for at least half a year(No.2).

 After my son entered kindergarten, his writing shocked me. I regretted that I should teach him to write alphabets and numbers earlier so that he could practice it in preschool. From his point of view, writing was just like drawing, free lines or shapes. I used to focus on his reading of numbers or alphabets, overlooking his writing. So my suggestion is that parents should also be concerned about their children's standard writing(No. 3).

My son encountered many problems in school, like misbehaviors owing to his summer birth, no much attention on teachers, and inaccurate spelling. The teachers input new words by means of phonetics, so my son spelled the words according to their pronunciation. He made mistakes in some words with special forms, like silent letters and voiced and voiceless pairs of consonants. So parents who decided to intervene with their children's literacy learning should pay more attention to their correct spelling(No. 5).

Summary

In-depth interviews were conducted with eight participants whose children studied in public kindergarten or primary school of a southern city in the United States. The study was guided by four research questions, which were addressed through 16 interview questions. The study employed purposive sampling to ensure that four samples were immigrant families and the other four were Chinese international students and visiting scholars.

Six themes emerged from the study, with related subthemes. They were Parents' Roles in Children's School

Readiness, Major Factors Effective in Children's School Readiness, Parental Involvement in Children's School Readiness, Practices in Conquering Barriers in Children's School Readiness, Factors that Affect Chinese Parents' Involvement, and Suggestions Concerning Children's School Readiness. Themes and subthemes were elaborated and the relationships among the themes, interview questions, and research questions were noted. Owing to the qualitative approach and the contextual nature of the questions, multiple themes were linked to research questions. Interview excerpts were cited to describe the themes and to supply with the richness of data from the exploratory and qualitative interviews.

Chapter 5
Discussion, Conclusions, Implications, and Recommendations

Issues of school readiness and kindergarten entry have been identified in educational research and practice since the middle of the twentieth century, and dominating educational practices of early childhood in the twenty-first century. School readiness functions as both a national educational aim and a local priority as well. Viewpoints regarding kindergarten readiness have often shed light on the perceptions of school administrators or early childhood educators.

This case study was designed to explore the perceptions of Chinese parents about their children's school readiness in five domains and to determine their involvement in their children's preparation for kindergarten guided by their belief. Through the use of a case study, perceptions and involvement of Chinese parents were examined by a series of in-depth interviews designated to demonstrate the

Chapter 5 Discussion, Conclusions, Implications, and Recommendations

following research questions:

1. How do Chinese parents perceive their role in their children's school readiness and preparation for kindergarten?

2. What are the major factors Chinese parents consider to be effective in their children's school readiness and preparation for kindergarten?

3. What are strategies and practices that Chinese parents employ in their children's school readiness and preparation for kindergarten?

4. What are the factors that affect Chinese parents' involvement in their children's school readiness and preparation for kindergarten?

Discussion of Core Themes

The participants responded to sixteen interview questions and agreed with recording, transcription, coding, and analysis using case study data analysis approach. The data sets unveiled themes and subthemes. The analysis produced six themes demonstrating participants' perceptions and involvement in their children's school readiness and preparation for kindergarten.

Theme 1: parents' roles in children's school readiness

The first theme was Chinese parents' roles in preparing their children for kindergarten. Participants reported beliefs regarding their roles as guide, supporter, facilitator, helper, fellow, and advocate for their children's preparation for kindergarten at home, at school, and in community. They described their efforts at their children's educational careers. Vygotsky's (1978) social constructivist theory of child development built a framework for a clear understanding of young children's development and appropriate developmental instruction. Chinese parents' roles as helpers in their children's preparation for kindergarten were in consistence with the notion "the zone of proximal development". They functioned to approach child's experience and move the child to a higher level of thinking than what the child could achieve independently. In addition, the social constructivist theory of child development pointed to the importance of young children as active participants in the learning process. So the participants acted as helpers in their children's learning and development rather than dictators. They helped their children to actively explore the world and enrich their understanding.

This finding is in consistence with the previous literature. For the participants in this study, parental roles and responsibility translated into being highly engaged with their children's school readiness, including arranging a variety of activities that highlighted children's preparation

Chapter 5 Discussion, Conclusions, Implications, and Recommendations

for kindergarten. This finding is supported by previous research which noted that parental involvement is one of the most important pieces of school readiness. A stable and secure home environment and parental involvement in educational opportunities were figured out as factors that influenced formal school readiness in positive ways. Home environment that encouraged learning and reading activities resulted in active parent-child interaction.

Theme 2: major factors effective in children's school readiness

In reaction to the major factors effective in children's school readiness, the participants mentioned personality of child, maturity, age, and gender, peers, school-related teaching strategies, united and supportive school environment, and family involvement.

As a piece of developmental view, issues of youngness and oldness, boys and girls were mentioned by most participants. They indicated that having a summer birthday would be a detriment to most of the young children upon their entry into kindergarten. This finding is not supported by the previous research that has been conducted on the difference of age. Morrison et al. (1997) found results that younger first graders progressed in a similar manner compared with their older peers. The inconsistency in the result is partly because the previous research focused on the children's academic performance. Instead, the participants of this study reported more of their concerns on children's behavioral problems. And they also admitted that although the children with summer birthday were confronted with many problems in adaptation to the kindergarten environment, they eventually got rid of these barriers when given more time and efforts from parents and teachers.

Beliefs concerning gender and school readiness figured prominently among the participants. They reported their beliefs that boys were more likely not to be ready for kindergarten than girls. The prevalence of the belief is not supported by some researchers. For instance, Marshall (2003) indicated that parents often believed in some outdated assumptions like the belief that boys are developed behind girls about six months to one year. The participants of this study believed that some boys had difficulties in following the behavioral expectations of kindergarten like sitting still and paying attention.

Among the factors effective in young children's school readiness, peers, the school strategies, environment and parental involvement took a larger part in the participants' responses. According to Bronfenbrenner (1986), ecological systems theory regarded development of young children within a system of connected environment. The micro-, meso-, exo-, and macro-levels of environment around the child were one of the important parts of the contextual nature of the study. School readiness was embedded in contexts of family, school, and larger community.

The micro-level issues involve the everyday, immediate

Chapter 5 Discussion, Conclusions, Implications, and Recommendations

family involvement in their children's school readiness. The meso-level issues were clearly shown by notes regarding the practices of schools. Most of the participants mentioned the significance of children's preschool experiences in shaping school readiness and preparation for kindergarten. Bronfenbrenner (1986) specifically noted the impact of preschool and peers on the family and on the shaping of the development of individual child. The exo-level issues involved the school district policies about kindergarten expectations. No participants noted the related opinion. The macro-level issues included the role of community in promoting children's development by offering multiple resources and interconnection among families and schools. American values about independence and assertiveness guided the state policies which accelerated the establishment of community services and resources. The community services and resources were macro-level considerations that parents believed to directly affect children's preparation for kindergarten. All the participants noted that they made use of some community services and resources in preparing their children for kindergarten.

Theme 3: parental involvement in children's school readiness

Participants described school readiness as a concept consisting of many different pieces including academic, emotional, developmental, and behavioral aspects. According to the NEGP (1990), the areas of school readiness included physical well-being and motor development, social and emotional development, approaches toward learning, language development, and cognition and general knowledge. The participants presented their strategies and practices in these five domains.

In physical well-being and motor development, the participants afforded physical exercise guided by parents, sports equipment, nutritious meals, nutrient supplements, adaptation to new rules of school, and a lot of resources and activities in the neighboring community. In social and emotional development, the participants mentioned companionship, encouragement, not too much attention, diverse family members, messages, parent-teacher conferences, volunteering, preparation for items for parties, attending parties, play dates, family dates, playmate, playground, early entry into preschool, a variety of extracurricular classes, and visits to libraries, bookstores, and museums. In approaches toward learning, the participants mentioned encouragement, check of folder, reading, books, art crafts, bed stories, homework, community resources, and preschool. In language development, the participants mentioned reading, communication with teachers, school activities, the implementation of reading plan, picture storybooks, e-products, Chinese environment, library, Chinese class, and English class. In cognition and general knowledge, the participants mentioned questions & answers, reading, math games, math training, and math in daily life.

Epstein(1995) noted the six types of parental involvement,

Chapter 5 Discussion, Conclusions, Implications, and Recommendations

including parenting, communication, participating in school activities, home learning environment, decision making, and community-related connection. The six types of parental involvement covered all the strategies and practices that the participants employed in the five domains of children's development regarding school readiness. On the basis of Epstein's framework, the six types of involvement have been categorized into three dimensions: home-based involvement, school-based involvement, and home-school conferencing. The finding of this study is consistent with many recent researches that have extensively applied the three dimensions into examination of parental involvement (Wanders et al., 2007).

Home-based involvement consists of a wide range of education-related activities at home, like providing rich literacy home environment, helping in coursework, and talking about school and academic expectations with their children. School-based involvement encompasses parents' assistance in classroom and actively engaging in workshops or other special events. Home-school conferencing acts as a linkage between home and school, like attending parent-teacher conferences, and interacting with teachers in terms of children's problems and progress.

This study connected Bronfenbrenner's ecological framework with the various types of parental involvement. Home-based involvement consists of part of the microsystem in children development. School-based involvement and parent-school conferencing constitute part of the mesosystem.

Theme 4: practices in conquering barriers in children's school readiness

The real development of the children mostly couldn't coincide with their parents' expectations. When it came to the ways to alleviate the barriers, the participants mentioned gradual adjustment, no much pressure, encouragement, lower expectations, rescheduling, rules establishment, and enrichment of parents.

Although some participants felt frustrated when encountering unexpected performance of their children, they hesitated to adopt tough exercise or negative comments. Instead, they would rather encourage their children and afford more flexible time and patience for their children's development. What is more, they try to review their own practices and enrich themselves in multiple ways. From the perspective of Vygotsky(1978), children are active participants in their acquisition and development, not being forced to attain information and knowledge. Parents make great efforts to support their children's learning and development, not acting as a dictator.

Theme 5: factors that affect Chinese parents' involvement

The participants noted that parental involvement in young children's development was crucial and the factors that influenced parental involvement included parental

Chapter 5 Discussion, Conclusions, Implications, and Recommendations

perceptions, individual characteristics of the child, natural development of the child, parents' peers, and family environment.

All the parents figured out the close correlations between parental perceptions and involvement. This finding is supported by studies which stated that family involvement turns to be an important piece of school readiness(Halliburton & Thornburg, 2004). And a safe and stable family environment and parental awareness in parental involvement in educational opportunities have been listed as factors that influenced kindergarten readiness in positive ways. Family environment that encouraged learning and reading activities were found to be crucial factors in school readiness. Research supports the beliefs of the parents that parental perceptions influence parental practices, which would boost school readiness.

Theme 6: suggestions concerning children's school readiness

After self-examination upon parental practices by the participants, they mentioned consistent education, natural development, specific practices for individual child, show and tell, physical development, knowledge base, literacy, spelling, and writing. Many participants have only one child, so they explored their practices and determined the efficiency according to their children's performance. After reviewing their practices, they realized both positive and negative effects of these practices. They suggested that children's development be a natural process and young children should adapt to the kindergarten environment with parents' support and encouragement more easily. However, little attention to children's literacy skills might lead to young children's lagging academic performance. Hence, parents should pay more attention to the extent to which they can get involved in their children's development.

Conclusions

Several conclusions could be drawn from the findings of the study, associating with the areas explored by the research questions, and framed within the participants' perspective. These conclusions included the importance of school readiness, shifted values in parental perceptions, correlations between parental perceptions and involvement, reading and readiness, and suggested forms of parental involvement in children's school readiness.

The importance of school readiness

A conclusion of the study is that school readiness was very important to the parents. School readiness was regarded as a real construct in early childhood realm, which could be demonstrated in terms of actual attitudes and behaviors of children. For the participants, all forms of education were of great importance, starting with preschool and continuing through children's educational

Chapter 5 Discussion, Conclusions, Implications, and Recommendations

life.

The importance of school readiness was also illustrated as the participants discussed their beliefs concerning early childhood education and their expectation for children's preparation for kindergarten. What is more, school readiness's importance was reflected in the intensity of strategies and practices the participants employed when preparing their children for kindergarten. They related to their own responsibility for assisting and encouraging readiness at home, cooperating with teachers, and offering more extracurricular activities in the community.

Shifted values in parental perceptions

All the parents regarded their children's physical health and well-being as the most important factor for a smooth transition to kindergarten. They attached importance to their children's physical size, getting enough rest, having a balanced diet, and abilities to perform self-help skills (e. g., eating, dressing, washing hands, and toileting independently). This finding might have implications for the shifted value that Chinese parents place more emphasis on their children's overall well-being and essential everyday living skills than on their academic skills. That is, Chinese parents of young children may give priority to children's physical health and well-being routines.

Meanwhile, the finding indicated that the participants also highlighted their children's social competence and emotional maturity, such as organizing outings with peers, communicating with teachers and children, ability to separate from parents, and positive attitude concerning going to school. Results of the current study are consistent with earlier literature (Dockett & Perry, 1999; West, et al., 1995). Although many participants realized the importance of emotional maturity and social competence for their children's entry into kindergarten, they did not connect to issues like boys starting kindergarten a year later than girls. Chinese parents may base their views upon their own personal experience and they believe that young boys will eventually adapt to the life in kindergarten, or higher grades. Furthermore, all the parents reported language skills as being important to their children's successful transition to kindergarten. These findings supported earlier studies that noted that parents did not focus more on academic skills than they did on social skills, emotional maturity, language skills, and physical development (Piotrkowksi, et al., 2001; Wesley & Buysse, 2003). The findings appear to suggest that Chinese parents begin to have a broader understanding about what is important for children's smooth transition to kindergarten and that it entails much more than the exact abilities to recognize letter, count to ten, and identify shapes and colors.

Correlations between parental perceptions and involvement

In accordance with the results of the fifth theme, all

Chapter 5 Discussion, Conclusions, Implications, and Recommendations

the participants indicated that their parental perceptions were highly connected with their strategies and practices. This is in consistence with the dominant philosophical principles in China that different viewpoints of world lead to different behaviors. The result suggests that the more important Chinese parents perceived the practices to be, the more frequently they did them. Simply, Chinese parents did what they perceived to be important. For instance, the participants valued young children's physical development and reading environment. These beliefs, in turn, were associated with their reported level of practices concerning their children's physical development and reading environment.

Reading and readiness

In young children's cognitive, language, and literacy skills development, the participants highly valued the function of reading. A conclusion is that Chinese parents relate reading to their children's language, cognitive, and literacy skills development. In addition to the teaching of preschool teachers in alphabetic knowledge and phonics, the participants conducted lots of reading activities with their children at home.

Suggested forms of parental involvement in children's school readiness

In order to promote young children's development in

multiple domains and prepare them ready for kindergarten, Chinese parents in the United States of America are suggested to establish home environments to support children, work out effective forms of school-to-home and home-to-school communication concerning school programs and young children's progress, volunteer to help and support school activities, acquire information and ideas regarding how to help students with homework at home and other curriculum-related planning and activities, volunteer to become parent leaders and representatives and become involved in school decisions, and identify and integrate services and resources from the community to strengthen school programs, parental practices, and children learning and development. In the first type of parental involvement, Chinese parents could take part in workshops, training programs, and online courses on parenting and young child rearing at each age and grade level. They ought to attach importance to health, nutrition, and other services. They could also join in some neighborhood meetings to help them understand schools. In this way, they will attain understanding of and confidence about parenting, child development, and changes in home conditions for learning and development as young children proceed through school. In addition, they tend to build up awareness of their challenges and obtain a feeling of support from other parents, school, and the community.

In communicating, Chinese parents could try to have conferences with teachers at least once a year with follow-

Chapter 5 Discussion, Conclusions, Implications, and Recommendations

ups, check daily folders of child work sent from school for review and comments, take notice of regular schedule of useful memos, phone calls, newsletter, and other communication, and get access to clear information on choosing courses, programs, and activities within schools and on all school policies, programs, transitions, and reforms. In this case, they can easily understand school policies and programs, monitor child's progress, respond effectively to child's problems, and interact with teachers efficiently.

In volunteering, Chinese parents could help teachers, students, other parents, and administrators in school and classroom volunteer program, work in parent room or family center for volunteer work, meetings, and resources for families, provide all families with needed information as class parents, telephone tree, or other structure, and aid safety and operation of school programs as parent patrols or other activities. Accordingly, Chinese parents will understand teacher's job, increase comfort in school, carry over school activities at home and establish self-confidence about the ability to work in school and with children, get awareness that families are welcome and valued at school, and have gains in specific skills of volunteer work.

In learning at home, Chinese parents could obtain information about homework policies and how to monitor and discuss schoolwork at home, get to know how to assist children to improve skills on development in five domains, complete regular schedule of homework that requires children to discuss and interact with parents, have calendars with activities for parents and students at home, and take part in family math, science, and reading activities at home. In this way, they become to know how to support, encourage, and help children at home, discuss with children about life in school, understand the instructional program each year, appreciate teaching skills, and get awareness of child as a learner.

In decision making, Chinese parents could make use of networks to connect all families with parent representatives and get information on school or local elections for school representatives. Afterwards, Chinese parents can have input into policies that affect their child's education, get a feeling of ownership of school, become aware of parents' voices in school decisions, and have shared experiences and connections with other families.

In collaborating with the community, Chinese parents could get information on cultural, recreational, social support, community health, and other programs or services, get access to community activities that relate to learning skills and talents, such as summer camps for children, enjoy service to the community near families, including art, music, recycling, drama, sports, and so on, and participate alumni in school programs for children. Therefore, they can be informed of knowledge and use of local resources so as to improve talents and skills or to get needed services. In addition, they can increase interactions

Chapter 5 Discussion, Conclusions, Implications, and Recommendations

with other families in community activities.

Implications

This study was designated with a qualitative methodology to unveil Chinese parents' perceptions and involvement in their children's school readiness. Implications in this section associate the conclusions of the study to early childhood educators, to incoming Chinese parents, and to community sources, in consistence with the ecological systems framework in the study.

Implications for preschool programming and kindergarten programming

School readiness was viewed as important and complex to many participants in the study across many dimensions. The implication is that preschool programs are the major sources of readiness and preparation, especially for Chinese families. Preschools may be viewed by some parents as goal-oriented towards school readiness, instead of an experience-based type of program. Early childhood educators have an opportunity or even a responsibility to re-frame preschool curricula as readiness curricula. Preschool education could be regarded as a part of the whole educational career of a child, and not as merely a pre-school. More focus on preschool education as it relates to kindergarten is one of the implications of this study.

The implication for early childhood educators is that Chinese parents of young children haven't narrowed their emphasis solely on the acquisition of cognitive skills in preschool. This implication is encouraging the adherence to the developmentally appropriate practice principle of early childhood education. Preschools can include all areas of development instead of highlighting specific skills.

All the participants laid much value on reading skills, both as a necessity for school readiness and a kindergarten educational goal as well. The implication is that reading skills are a necessity at the preschool level for school readiness. Purposive planning for development of early literacy skills and combination of literacy activities in preschools were expected by the participants. Consistency of goals in relation with the timing of the input of reading skills, the use of approaches like phonetic instruction, and the assessment of reading skills before kindergarten entry are all considerations when designing preschool activities that meet the needs of both parents and children.

The involvement of Chinese parents concerning readiness was a major finding of the study. The participants viewed their early practices and incorporation with preschool as crucial to their children's development. Some parents, however, were confronted with the lack of information regarding their specific practices, with limited guidance from preschool or kindergarten. More communication between teachers and parents and dissemination of information

Chapter 5 Discussion, Conclusions, Implications, and Recommendations

could occur in preschools in order to better meet Chinese parents' needs.

Chinese parental perceptions regarding the unsuitability of their children, especially Chinese children lack of fluent English and boys with summer date birth, suggests that the image of kindergarten has two aspects. Either children are not able to be completely prepared for kindergarten environment, or kindergarten itself is not adequately prepared for a wide range of students and is not specifically planned to meet the needs of students of diverse cultural backgrounds and young boys. It implied that kindergarten professionals, both classroom teachers and administrators, can explore ways to adjust to young children's typical developmental stages and to discuss the appropriateness of kindergarten environment to Chinese parents, especially parents of young boys.

Compared with holding-back, some parents believed that practices like bridge programming was preferred by younger children in need of more maturity. Both preschool professionals and kindergarten professionals could work together to explore the content and goals of bridge programs, and verify the utility of bridge programs.

Implications for incoming Chinese parents

Regarding school readiness as a family issue instead of entirely focusing on child or program components is one of the implications of the study. Family practices appeared as an important source of children's preparation for kindergarten. Parents who had specific knowledge and experience concerning kindergarten programs shared their knowledge with peers. Utilizing the expertise of these parents who have direct knowledge of parental involvement in school readiness is an area of examination and exploration for early childhood educators. Experienced parents could be viewed as resources and mentors to other inexperienced preschool parents as they sought useful strategies and practices in their children's school readiness.

The parental role in school readiness was a main finding of the study, and an implication is that the participants regarded themselves as helpers to their children and partners with preschools. Participants made great efforts to ensure their children's preparation for kindergarten by working with the children at home, enrolling their children in preschool programs, and making use of community resources. Determining specific home activities to promote school readiness could be helpful in facilitating home/school connections for school readiness.

On the basis of the findings of the study, parents should speak Chinese as much as possible at home. The parents should not worry about their children's English development in that they have the ideal language environment. Chinese development will never occur once English turns to be the dominant home language. Immigrant Chinese parents should interact with their

Chapter 5   Discussion, Conclusions, Implications, and Recommendations

children concerning the importance of learning Chinese and visit China regularly to improve their children's Chinese language proficiency.

All the family members need to work together as a team and keep consistent in parenting practices. They also must make it clear to children that all the members share the same beliefs and practices.

Implications for community sources

All the participants of the study explored their use of community sources in preparing their children for kindergarten in five domains, including playground, library, museum, and extracurricular programs. The implication for community sources is that the community should establish more public facilities to aid the development of young children in multiple domains and plan more specific activities for children of diverse cultural backgrounds. In this way, Chinese children who just start their study and life in the United States can practice English more, make more friends, and maintain their social and emotional development.

Recommendations for future research

On the basis of the discussions, conclusions, and implications of this study, the following recommendations for future research are suggested:

1. Future research efforts should emphasize larger

sample sizes and include Chinese parents in other places in the U. S. to verify whether there exist significant differences in parental perceptions between parents of boys and girls, fathers and mothers, and parents of gifted and average students. Future research should include parents with different socioeconomic status, as well as different generations.

2. Only data from parents were examined in the study, and data from children will be desirable in the future research. In order to help and improve children's school readiness, researchers should not only attain parental perceptions and practices, but children's perceptions and practices as well.

3. A longitudinal study should be also carried out for future research so as to verify whether parental perceptions and involvement vary as children grow older.

References

Arnold, D. H., Zeljo, A., Doctoroff, G. L., & Ortiz, C. (2008). Parent involvement in preschool: Predictors and the relation of involvement to pre-literacy development. *School Psychology Review,* 37(1), 74.

Association for Qualitative Research. (2011). *Qual research recruitment checklist*. Retrieved from http://www.aqr.org.uk/refsection/recruitment-checklist.shtml.

Aunola, K., Leskinen, E., Lerkkanen, M. K., &Nurmi, J. E.(2004). Developmental dynamics of math performance from preschool to Grade 2. *Journal of Educational Psychology,* 96(4), 699.

Ballantyne, K. G., Sanderman, A. R., & McLaughlin, N. (2008). Dual language learners in the early years: Getting ready to succeed in school. Washington, DC: National Clearinghouse for English language learners. Retrieved from http://www.ncela.gwu.edu/resabout/ccell/earlyyears.pdf.

Bronfenbrenner, U. (1986). Ecology of the family as a context for human development: Research perspectives. *Developmental Psychology,* 22(6), 723.

Brooks, J. (2011). *The Process of Parenting.* Boston, MA: McGraw-Hill.

Brooks-Gunn, J., &Markman, L. B. (2005). The contribution of parenting to ethnic and racial gaps in school readiness. *The Future of Children,* 75 (1), 139-168.

Chao, R. K. (1994). Beyond parental control and authoritarian parenting style: Understanding Chinese parenting through the cultural notion of training. *Child Development,* 65(4), 1111-1119.

Chao, R. K. (1996). Chinese and European American mothers' beliefs about the role of parenting in children's school success. *Journal of Cross-Cultural Psychology,* 27, 403-423.

Chao, R. K. (2001). Extending research on the consequences of parenting style for Chinese Americans and European Americans. *Child Development,* 72(6), 1832-1843.

Chen, X. (1998). The changing Chinese family: Resources, parenting practices, and children's socio-emotional problems. *Family and Family Therapy in International Perspective.* Milan, Italy: Marinelli Editrice.

Coleman, J. S. (1966). *Equality of educational opportunity.* Washington, DC: U. S. Office of Education.

Connell, C. M., & Prinz, R. J. (2002). The impact of

References

childcare and parent-child interactions on school readiness and social skills development for low-income African American children. *Journal of School Psychology*, 40(2), 177–193.

Creswell, J. W. (2003). *Research design: Qualitative, quantitative, and mixed methods approaches* (2nd ed.). United States of America Library of Congress Cataloging-in-Publication. SAGE Publications.

Creswell, J. W. (2008). *Research design: Qualitative, quantitative, and mixed methods approaches* (3rd ed.). Thousand Oaks, CA: SAGE.

Creswell, J. W. (2008). *Educational research: Planning, conducting, and evaluating quantitative and qualitative research* (3rd ed.). Upper Saddle River, NJ: Pearson, Merrill Prentice Hall.

Eccles, J. S., & Harold, R. D. (1996). Family involvement in children's and adolescents' schooling. In J. S. Eccles & R. D. Harold(Eds.), *Family-school links: How do they affect educational outcomes?* (pp. 3–34). Hillsdale, NJ: Erlbaum.

Egertson, H. A. (1987). *The shifting kindergarten curriculum*. ERIC Digest: ERIC Clearinghouse on Elementary and Early Childhood Education. Office of Educational Research and Improvement, U. S. Department of Education. Retrieved from http://readvweb.crc.uiuc.edu/library/pre1990/egertson.html.

Entwisle, D. (1995). The role of schools in sustaining early childhood program benefits. *Future Child,* 58, 133-144.

Epstein, J. L. (1995). School/family/community partnerships: Caring for the children we share. *Phi Delta Kappan,* 76(9), 701-712.

Epstein, J. L., & Sheldon, S. B. (2002). Present and accounted for: Improving student attendance through family and community involvement. *The Journal of Educational Research,* 95(5), 308-318.

Faires, J., Nichols, W. D., & Rickelman, R. J. (2000). Effects of parental involvement in developing competent readers in first grade. *Reading Psychology,* 21 (3), 195-215.

Fan, X., & Chen, M. (2001). Parental involvement and students' academic achievement: A meta-analysis. *Educational Psychology,* 13(1), 1-22.

Fantuzzo, J., McWayne, C., & Bulotsky, R. (2003). Forging strategic partnerships to advance mental health science and practice for vulnerable children. *School Psychology Review,* 32, 17-37.

Fantuzzo, J., McWayne, C., Perry, M. A., & Childs, S. (2004). Multiple dimensions of family involvement and their relations to behaviors and learning competencies for urban, low-income children. *School Psychology Review,* 33(4), 467-480.

Fantuzzo, J., Tighe, E., & Childs, S. (2000). Family involvement questionnaire: A multivariate assessment of family participation in early childhood education. *Journal of Educational Psychology,* 92(2), 367–376.

Farver, J. M., Xu, Y., Eppe, S., & Lonigan, C. J. (2006). Home environments and young Latino children's school readiness. *Early Childhood Research Quarterly,* 21, 196–212.

Gee, J. (2004). *Situated language and learning.* New York, NY: Routledge.

Gill, S., & Reynolds, A. J. (1999). Educational expectations and school achievement of urban African American children. *Journal of School Psychology.* Special Issue: Schooling and High Risk Populations: The Chicago Longitudinal Study, 37, 403–424.

Graue, M. E. (1992). Social interpretations of readiness for kindergarten. *Early Childhood Research Quarterly,* 7(2), 225–243.

Graue, M. E., Kroeger, J., & Brown, C. (2003). The gift of time: Enactments of developmental thought in early childhood practice. *Early Childhood Research and Practice,* 5(1). Retrieved from http://ecrp.uiuc.edu/v5nl/graue.html.

Green, C. L., Walker, J. M., Hoover-Dempsey, K. V., & Sandler, H. M. (2007). Parents' motivations for involvement in children's education: An empirical test of a theoretical model of parental involvement. *Journal of Educational Psychology,* 99(3), 532.

Grolnick, W. S., Friendly, R. W., & Bellas, V. M. (2009).

Parenting and children's motivation at school. In K. R. Wenzel & A. Wigfield (Eds.), *Handbook of motivation at school* (pp. 279 - 300). New York, NY: Routledge/Taylor & Francis.

Grolnick, W. S., & Slowiaczek, M. L. (1994). Parents' involvement in children's schooling: A multi-dimensional conceptualization and motivational model. *Child Development,* 65(1), 237 - 252.

Hair, E., Halle, T., Terry-Humen, E., Lavelle, B., & Calkins, J. (2006). Children's school readiness in the ECLS-K: Predictions to academic, health, and social outcomes in first grade. *Early Childhood Research Quarterly,* 21(4), 431 - 454.

Harkness, S., & Super, C. M. (Eds.). (1996). *Parents' cultural belief systems: Their origins, expressions and consequences*. New York, NY: Guilford.

Head Start. (2011). *Head Start Approach to Readiness*. HHS/ACF/OHS.

Heine, S. J., Kitayama, S., Lehman, D. R., Takata, T., Ide, E., Leung, C, et al. (2001). Divergent consequences of success and failure in Japan and North America: An investigation of self-improving motivations and malleable selves. *Journal of Personality and Social Psychology,* 81, 599 - 615.

High/Scope Educational Research Foundation. (2006). *From implementation to impact: An evaluation of the South Carolina First Steps to School Readiness Program:*

References

2006. Ypsilanti, MI: Author.

Hill, N. E., & Taylor, L. C. (2004). Parental school involvement and children's academic achievement. *Current Directions in Psychological Sciences,* 13(4), 161–164.

Hirsh-Pasek, K. (1991). Pressure or challenge in preschool: How academic environments affect children. In Rescorla, L., Hyson, M., &Hirsh-Pasek, K., editors. *Academic instruction in early childhood: Challenge or pressure?* San Francisco, CA: Jossey-Bass.

Hirschman, C., & Wong, M. G. (1986). The extraordinary educational attainment of Asian-Americans: A search for historical evidence and explanations. *Social Forces,* 65, 1–27.

Ho, D. Y. F.(1986). Chinese patterns of socialization: A critical review. In M. H. Bond(Ed.), *The Psychology of the Chinese people* (pp.1–37). Hong Kong: Oxford University Press.

Ho, S. C. (1995). Parent Involvement: A comparison of different definitions and explanations. *Education Journal,* 23(1), 39–68.

Holloway, S. D., Yamamoto, Y., Suzuki, S., &Mindnich, J. D.(2008). Determinants of parental involvement in early schooling: Evidence from Japan. *Early Childhood Research & Practice,* 10(1). Retrieved from http://ecrp.uiuc.edu/v10n1/holloway.html.

Hoover-Dempsey, K. V., Battiato, A. C., Walker, J. M.

T., Reed, R. P., Dejong, J. M., & Jones, K. P. (2001). Parental involvement in homework. *Educational Psychologist*, 36(3), 195-210.

Hoover-Dempsey, K. V., & Sandler, H. M. (1997). Why do parents become involved in their children's education? *Review of Educational Research*, 67(1), 3-42.

Huntsinger, C. S., Jose, P. E., Larson, S. L., Balsink Krieg, D., & Shaligram, C. (2000). Mathematics, vocabulary, and reading development in Chinese American and European American children over the primary school years. *Journal of Educational Psychology*, 92(4), 745.

Huntsinger, C. S., Larson, S. L., & Krieg, D. B. (1998). *Mathematics and vocabulary development in Chinese American and European American children over the primary school years*. Paper presented at the Annual Meeting of the American Educational Research Association. San Diego, CA. (ERIC Document Reproduction Service No. ED 422445)

Janus, M., & Offord, D. R. (2007). Development and psychometric properties of the Early Development Instrument (EDI): A measure of children's school readiness. *Canadian Journal of Behavioral Science*, 39(1), 1-22.

Jeynes, W. H. (2003). A meta-analysis of the effects of parental involvement on minority children's academic achievement. *Education and Urban Society*, 35(2),

202-218.

Jeynes, W. H. (2005). A meta-analysis of the relation of parental involvement to urban elementary school student academic achievement. *Urban Education,* 40 (3), 237-269.

Jeynes, W. H. (2007). The Relationship between Parental Involvement and Urban Secondary School Student Academic Achievement A Meta-Analysis. *Urban Education,* 42(1), 82-110.

Jose, P. E., Huntsinger, C. S., Huntsinger, P. R., & Liaw, F. R. (2000). Parental values and practices relevant to young children's social development in China (Taiwan Province) and the United States. *Journal of Cross-Cultural Psychology,* 31(6), 677-702.

Jstice, L. M., Bowles, R. P., Pence Turnbull, K. L., & Skibbe, L. E. (2007). Promoting academic and social-emotional school readiness: The Head Start REDI program. *Child Development,* 79(6), 460-476.

Kagan, S. L. (1992). Readiness past, present, and future: Shaping the agenda. *Young Children,* 48(1), 48-53.

Kagan, S. L., Moore, E., & Bredekamp, S. (1995). *Reconsidering children's early learning and development: Toward shared beliefs and vocabulary.* Washington, DC: National Education Goals Panel.

Kavale, K. A. (1996). *Interviews: An introduction to qualitative research interviewing.* Thousand Oaks, CA: SAGE.

Kerr, D. (2004). Family transformations and the well-being of children: Recent evidence from Canadian longitudinal data. *Journal of Comparative Family Studies*, 35, 73-87.

Kim, E. J., Im, H. S., Nahm, E. Y., & Hong, S. H. (2012). Korean American parents' reconstruction of immigrant parenting in the United States. *Journal of Cultural Diversity*, 19(4), 124-132.

Kim, J., Murdock, T., & Choi, D. (2005). Investigation of parents' beliefs about readiness for kindergarten: An examination of National Household Education Survey (NHES: 93). *Educational Research Quarterly*, 29(2), 3-17.

Kingston, S., Huang, K. Y., Calzada, E., Dawson-McClure, S., & Brotman, L. (2013). Parent involvement in education as a moderator of family and neighborhood socio-economic context on school readiness among young children. *Journal of Community Psychology*, 41(3), 265-276.

Kohl, G. O., Lengua, L. J., & McMahon, R. J. (2000). Parent involvement in school conceptualizing multiple dimensions and their relations with family and demographic risk factors. *Journal of School Psychology*, 38(6), 501-523.

Laforett, D. R., & Mendez, J. L. (2010). Parent involvement, parental depression, and program satisfaction among low-income parents participating in a two-generation early childhood education program. *Early Education and Development,* 21(4), 517 – 535.

Lather, P. (1992). Critical frames in educational research: Feminist and post-structural perspectives. *Theory into Practice,* 31(2), 87 – 99.

Lau, E. Y., Li, H., & Rao, N. (2011). Parental involvement and children's readiness for school in China. *Educational Research,* 53(1), 95 – 113.

Leedy, P. D., & Ormrod, J. E. (2010). *Practical research: Planning and design* (9th ed.). Upper Saddle River, NJ: Pearson.

Li, H., & Rao, N. (2000). Parental influences on Chinese literacy development: A comparison of preschoolers in China (Beijing, Hong Kong) and Singapore. *International Journal of Behavioral Development,* 24 (1), 82 – 90.

Li, J. (2005). Mind or virtue: Western and Chinese beliefs about learning. *Current Directions in Psychological Science,* 14, 190 – 194.

Lin, H. L., Lawrence, F. R., & Gorrell, J. (2003). Kindergarten teachers' views of children's readiness for school. *Early Childhood Research Quarterly,* 18(2), 225 – 237.

Luo, R., Tamis-LeMonda, C. S., & Song, L. (2013). Chinese parents' goals and practices in early childhood. *Early Childhood Research Quarterly,* 28 (4), 843 – 857.

Maccoby, E. E., & Martin, J. (1983). Socialization in the context of the family: Parent child interaction. In E. M. Hetherington (Ed.), *Handbook of child psychology: Vol. 4. Socialization, personality, and social development* (4th ed., pp. 1–101). New York, NY: John Wiley.

Markus, H. R., & Kitayama, S. (1991). Culture and the self: Implications for cognition, emotion, and motivation. *Psychological Review*, 98, 224–253.

Marshall, H. H. (2003). Opportunity deferred or opportunity taken? An updated look at delaying kindergarten entry. *Beyond the Journal*. Retrieved from http://www.naeyc.org/resources/joumal/beyond_trans.asp.

Marshall, M. N. (1996). Sampling for qualitative research. *Family Practice*, 13, 522–525. doi: 10.1093/fampra/13.6.522

Mashburn, A. J., & Pianta, R. C. (2006). Social relationships and school readiness. *Early Education and Development*, 17(1), 151–176.

McAllister, C. L., Wilson, P. C., Green, B. L., & Baldwin, J. L. (2005). Come and take a walk: Listening to early Head Start parents on school-readiness as a matter of child, family, and community health. *American Journal of Public Health*, 95(4), 617–625.

McWayne, C. M., Cheung, K., Wright, L. E. G., &Hahs-Vaughn, D. L. (2012). Patterns of school readiness among head start children: Meaningful within-group variability during the transition to kindergarten. *Journal of Educational Psychology,* 104 (3), 862.

Mehaffie, K. E., & Fraser, J. (2007). School readiness; Definitions, best practices, assessments, and cost. In C. J. Groark, K. E. Mehaffie, R. B. McCall, & M. T. Greenberg (Eds.), *Evidence-based practices and programs for early childhood care and education.* Thousand Oaks, CA: Corwin Press.

Merriam, S. B. (1998). *Qualitative research and case study applications in education.* San Francisco, CA: Jossey-Bass.

Miles, M. B., & Huberman, A. M. (1994). *Qualitative data analysis* (2nd ed.). London, UK: SAGE.

Mosby's Medical Dictionary. (2009). *Child development.* Retrieved from http://Mosbys-Medical-Dictionary-5th-ed/dp/0815146310.

Mostyn, B. (1985). The content analysis of qualitative research data: A dynamic approach. In M. Brenner, J. Brown & D. Cauter (Eds.), *The research interview* (pp. 115–145). London, UK: Academic Press.

National Association for the Education of Young Children. (2009). *Developmentally appropriate practice in early childhood programs serving children from birth through age 8.* Retrieved from http://www.naeyc.org/files/naeyc/file/positions/position%20statement%20Web.pdf.

National Association of School Psychologists. (2006). Effective parenting: Positive support for families.

NASP Position Statement. Retrieved from http://www. nasponline. org/about _ nasp/positionpapers/parenting. pdf.

National Center for Education Statistics. (2000). *Children who enter kindergarten late or repeat kindergarten: Their characteristics and later school performance*. Washington, DC: U. S. Department of Education.

National Center for Education Statistics. (2010). 2010 *National Household Education Survey (NHES:* 2010). Washington, DC: U. S. Department of Education.

National Education Association. (2015). *No Child Left Behind Act/ESEA*. Washington, DC: National Education Association. Retrieved from http://www. nea. org/esea/index. html.

National Education Goals Panel. (1995a). *Executive summary to the 1995 goals report: Improving education through family-school-community partnerships* (Technical Report No. 96 - 03). Washington, DC: U. S. Government Printing Office.

National Education Goals Panel. (1995b). *The National Education Goals report: Building a nation of learners*. Washington, DC: U. S. Department of Education.

National Household Education Survey School Readiness Survey. (1993). Retrieved from http://nces. ed. gov/nhes/surveytopics_early. asp.

Nelson, R. F. (2005). The impact of ready environments on achievement in kindergarten. *Journal of Research in Childhood Education*, 19(3), 215-221.

Neuman, W. L. (2006). *Social research methods: Qualitative and quantitative approaches* (6th ed.). Upper Saddle River, NJ: Prentice Hall.

Ng, F. F., Pomerantz, E. M., & Lam, S. F. (2007). European American and Chinese parents' responses to children's success and failure: Implications for children's responses. *Developmental Psychology*, 43, 1239-1255.

Okagaki, L., &Frensch, P. A. (1998). Parenting and children's school achievement: A multi-ethnic perspective. *American Educational Research Journal*, 35 (1), 123-144.

Olsen, G., & Fuller, M. (2012). *Home-school relations: Working successfully with parents and families* (4th ed.). Upper Saddle River, NJ: Pearson Education, Inc.

Parmar, P., Harkness, S., & Super, C. M. (2004). Asian and Euro-American parents' ethnotheories of play and learning: Effects on preschool children's home routines and school behavior. *International Journal of Behavioral Development*, 28, 97-104.

Patrikakou, E. N., Weissberg, R. P., Redding, S., & Walberg, H. J. (2005). School-family partnerships: Enhancing the academic, social, and emotional learning of children. In E. N. Patrikakou, R. P. Weissberg, S. Redding, & H. J. Walberg (Eds.), *School-family partnerships for children's success* (pp. 1 – 17). New York, NY: Teachers College Press.

Patton, M. Q. (2002). *Qualitative research and evaluation methods* (3rd ed.). Thousand Oaks, CA: SAGE.

Pelletier, J., & Brent, J. M. (2002). Parent participation in children's school readiness: The effects of parental self-efficacy, cultural diversity and teacher strategies. *International Journal of Early Childhood,* 34(1), 45 – 60.

Petrakos, H. H., & Lehrer, J. S. (2011). Parents' and teachers' perceptions of transition practices in kindergarten. *Exceptionality Education International,* 21 (2), 62 – 73.

Pianta, R. C., & Cox, M. J. (1999). *The transition to kindergarten*. Baltimore, MD: Paul H. Brookes.

Pianta, R. C., & Kraft-Sayre, M. (1999). Parents' observations about their children's transitions. *Young Children,* 54(3), 47 – 52.

Piotrowski, C. S., Botsko, M., & Matthews, E. (2000). Parents' and teachers' beliefs about children's school readiness in a high need community. *Early Childhood Research Quarterly,* 15(4), 537 – 558.

Ploeg, J. (1999). Identifying the best research design to fit the question: Part 2: qualitative design. *Evidence-Based Nursing,* 2, 36 – 37. doi: 10.1136/ebn.2.2.36

PNC Financial Services Group, Inc. (2007). *PNC study of early childhood education*. Retrieved from https://www.pnc.com/webapp/unsec/Requester?resource=/

References

wcm/resources/file/eb2e1343e2cbe74/PNCStudy_Parent TeacherFindings.pdf

Pomerantz, E. M., Moorman, E. A., & Litwack, S. D. (2007). The how, whom, and why of parents' involvement in children's academic lives: More is not always better. *Review of Educational Research*, 77(3), 373–410.

Pyle, R. R., Bates, M. P., Greif, J. L., & Furlong, M. J. (2005). School readiness needs of Latino preschoolers: A focus on parents' comfort with home-school collaboration. *The California School Psychologist*, 10, 105–116.

Rafoth, M. A., Buchenauer, E. L., Crissman, K. K., &Halko, J. L. (2004). *School Readiness—Preparing Children for Kindergarten and Beyond: Information for Parents*. Bethesda, MD: National Association of School Psychologists.

Rimm-Kaufman, S. E., & Pianta, R. C. (2000). An ecological perspective on the transition to kindergarten: A theoretical framework to guide empirical research. *Journal of Applied Developmental Psychology*, 21(5), 491–511.

Ritchie, S., Weiser, B., Kraft-Sayre, M., Mason, E., Crawford, G., & Howes, C. (2010). *Snapshot*. Chapel Hill, NC: University of North Carolina, Chapel Hill.

Rogers, T., Marshall, E. & Tyson, C. A. (2006). Dialogic narratives of literacy, teaching, and schooling: Preparing literacy teachers for diverse settings. *Reading Research Quarterly*, 41(2), 202–250.

Rosenkoetter, S., Schroeder, C., Rous, B., Hains, D. A., Shaw, J., & McCormick, K. (2009). *A Review of Research in Early Childhood Transition: Child and Family Studies Technical Report* # 5. Lexington: University of Kentucky, Human Development Institute, National Early Childhood Transition Center. Retrieved from http://www.ihdi.uky.edu/nectc

Russell, C. K., & Gregory, D. M. (2003). Evaluation of qualitative research studies. *Evidence-Based Nursing*, 6 (2), 36 - 40. doi: 10.1136/ebn.6.2.36

Schargel, F. P., & Smink, J. (2001). *Strategies to help solve our school dropout problem*. Larchmont, NY: Eye on Education.

Schneider, B., & Lee, Y. (1990). A model for academic success: The school and home environment of East Asian students. *Anthropology and Education Quarterly*, 21 (4), 358 - 377.

Seginer, R. (2006). Parents' educational involvement: A developmental ecology perspective. *Parenting: Science and Practice*, 6(1), 1 - 48.

Seidman, I. (2006). *Interviewing as qualitative research: A guide for researchers in education and the social sciences* (3rd ed.). New York, NY: Teachers College Press.

Seligman, M. (2000). *Conducting effective conferences with parents of children with disabilities*. New York, NY: Guilford Press.

Sénéchal, M., & LeFevre, J. A. (2002). Parental

involvement in the development of children's reading skill: A five-year longitudinal study. *Child Development,* 73(2), 445-460.

Shore, R. (1998). *Ready schools: A report of the Goal 1 Ready Schools Resource Group.* National Education Goals Panel. Retrieved on December 2, 2006 from www.negp.gov/Reports/readvsch.pdf.

Siu, S. F. (1996). *Report No. 8: Asian American students at risk: A literature review.* Retrieved from http://www.csos.ihu.edu/crespar/Reports/report08entire.html.

Sprenger, M. (2008). *The developing brain: Birth to age eight.* Thousand Oaks, CA: Corwin Press.

Stevenson, H. W., Stigler, J. W., Lee, S., Luker, G. W., Kitamura, S., & Hsu, C. (1985). Cognitive performance and academic achievement of Japanese, Chinese, and American children. *Child Development,* 56, 718-734.

Stone, S. (2006). Correlates of change in student reported parent involvement in schooling: A new look at the National Education Longitudinal Study of 1988. *American Journal of Orthopsychiatry,* 76(4), 518-530.

Swick, D. C. (2007). *The effects of parental involvement on children's school readiness skills.* (Doctoral dissertation). Retrieved from ProQuest Dissertations and Theses database. (Access Order No. AAT 3272704).

Taylor, L. C., Clayton, J. D., & Rowley, S. J. (2004).

Academic socialization: Understanding parental influences on children's school-related development in early years. *Review of General Psychology,* 8(3), 163 - 178.

Teale, W. H., & Sulzby, E. (1986). Introduction: Emergent literacy as a perspective for examining how young children become writers and readers. In W. H. Teale,& E. Sulzby (Eds.), *Emergent literacy: writing and reading.* Norwood, NJ: Albex.

Tobin, J. J., Wu, D. Y. H.,& Davidson, D. H. (1989). *Preschool in three cultures.* New Haven, CT: Yale University Press.

Tongco, M. D. (2007). Purposive sampling as a tool for informant selection. *A Journal of Plants, People, and Applied Research,* 5, 147 - 158. Retrieved from http://scholarspace. manoa. hawaii. edu/bitstream/handle/10125/227/1547 - 3465 - 05 - 147. pdf

Trumbull, E., & Rothstein-Fisch, C. (2011). The intersection of culture and achievement motivation. *The School Community Journal,* 21(2), 25 - 53.

Tsai, D. M. (1992). *Family impact on high achieving Chinese-American students: A qualitative analysis.* Unpublished doctoral dissertation, The University of Connecticut, Storrs, CT.

Tweed, R. G., & Lehman, D. R. (2002). Learning considered within a cultural context: Confucian and Socratic Approaches. *American Psychologist,* 57, 89 - 99.

U. S. Bureau of the Census. (2016). *U. S. Census Bureau*

delivers Nevada's 2010 census population totals, including first look at race and Hispanic origin data for legislative redistricting. Retrieved from http://www.census.gov/newsroom/releases/archives/2010_census/cb 11 -cn51.html

U. S. Census Bureau. (2016). *Educational attainment of the population 25 years and over by sex, for Asian alone or in combination and white alone, not Hispanic: 2015.* Retrieved from http://www.census.gov/hhes/socdemo/education/data/cps/2015/tables.html

U. S. Department of Education, *No Child Left Behind Act of* 2001. (2002). P. L. 107 – 110. Available online at http://www.nochildleftbehind.gov.

Vygotsky, L. S. (1978). *Mind in society: The development of higher psychological processes.* Cambridge, MA: Harvard University Press.

Walberg, H. J. (1984). Families as partners in educational productivity. *Phi Delta Kappan,* 65, 397 – 400.

Wanders, C., Mendez, J. L., & Downer, J. T. (2007). Parent characteristics economic stress and neighborhood context as predictors of parent involvement in preschool children education. *Journal of School Psychology,* 45(6), 619 – 636.

Wang, L., Li, X., & Li, N. (2014). Socio-economic status and mathematics achievement in China: a review. *The International Journal on Mathematics Education,* 46(7), 1051 – 1060.

Welsch, D. M., & Zimmer, D. M. (2008). After-School Supervision and Children's Cognitive Achievement. *The BE Journal of Economic Analysis and Policy*, 8(1), 1-27.

West, J., Denton, K., & Reaney, L. M. (2000). *The kindergarten year: Findings from the Early Childhood Longitudinal Study, Kindergarten class of 1998-1999* (Rep. No. NCES 2001023). Washington, DC: National Center for Education Statistics.

West, J., Germino-Hausken, E., & Collins, M. (1993). *Readiness for kindergarten: Parent and teacher beliefs. NCES* 93-257. Washington, DC: U. S. Department of Education, National Center for Education Statistics.

Wong, M. G. (1995). Chinese Americans. In P. G. Min(Ed.), *Asian Americans: Contemporary trends and issues* (pp.58-94). Thousand Oaks, CA: Sage Publications.

Wong, P., Lai, C. F., Nagasawa, R., & Lin, T. (1998). Asian Americans as a model minority: Self-perceptions and perceptions by other racial groups. *Social Perspectives*, 41(1), 95-118.

Xu, J. (2005, July). Preschool education. Paper presented at the 1st China Early Childhood Education Forum, Beijing, China.

Yeboah, D. A. (2002). Enhancing transition from early childhood phase to primary education: Evidence from the research literature. *Early Years*, 22(1), 51-68.

Yin, R. (2003). *Case study research: Design and methods* (3rd ed.). London: SAGE Publications.

Zhang, X., Sun, L., & Gai, X. (2008). Perceptions of teachers' and parents' regarding school readiness. *Frontiers of Education in China*, 3(3), 460–471.

Zhao, Y., & Qiu, W. (2009). How good are the Asians? Refuting four myths about Asian-American academic achievement. *Phi Delta Kappan* 90(5): 338–344.

Appendices

Appendix A: Cover Letter to Parents

Dear Parents,

The important topic of school readiness and Chinese parents' perceptions and involvement in preparation for kindergarten is being explored through this research study. This project involves Chinese parents of children whose ages range from pre-kindergarten through grade three.

My name is Xiaoli Sheng, and as an Ed. D. Candidate in the Early Childhood Education program at Jackson State University, I have a deep interest in school readiness issues. As a part of my doctoral studies, I am conducting a study regarding Chinese parents' perceptions and involvement in school readiness and inviting you to participate. My university advisor is Dr. Evornia Kincaid. You have showed interest in my topic in the church weekly fellowship.

Appendices

The study involves exploring Chinese parents' perceptions and involvement in school readiness through a single interview in a convenient, private setting. The interview is expected to last approximately one hour. The interview questions are open-ended; that is, they will consist of questions designed to allow you to freely express your perceptions and involvement about the topic. One of several interview settings will be available to you: at the investigator's office, in your home, or in a nearby private room.

Your participation is completely voluntary, and you should feel no pressure to participate. If you do agree to participate, I will contact you and schedule an interview. At the time of the interview, you will be asked to sign a form, "Consent Form for Research Participants". There are no direct benefits to you from participation in the study. Your responses will, however, provide research information about Chinese parents' perceptions and involvement in school readiness that may further understanding of how families respond to issues surrounding young children and school readiness.

As a participant, your confidentiality will be protected through the use of an alphanumeric code and private interview location. The interviews will be recorded and transcribed by me. The transcripts will then be analyzed by me as well as several reviewers, who will only identify the transcripts by the code number. The records and transcripts will be stored in a locked cabinet in my major professor's office, and all records and hard copies will be destroyed three years after the end of the study. Your participation is voluntary and you may withdraw at any point during the interview process. Should you feel fatigue or physical discomfort during the interview, you will be able to take breaks at any time.

I realize that the time of busy parents is valuable, and I would deeply appreciate the gift of about one hour of your time. If you would like to participate in this important research, please indicate your willingness by replying to this email. I will contact you by phone to arrange an interview time.

Thank you for your consideration about participation in this study. Please call me at _____ or send me emails via if you have any questions.

Sincerely yours,
Xiaoli Sheng

Appendix B: Consent Form

Jackson State University
Division of Research & Federal Relations

CONSENT FORM FOR RESEARCH PARTICIPANTS
Part I:
Section I: Investigator
Name: Xiaoli Sheng
Department: Elementary and Early Childhood Education
Address: 1703 Old Fannin Road Apt. F11
City, State, Zip Code: Flowood, MS 39232
Telephone Number: 601 - 874 - 4117
JSU Email Address: j00788990@students.jsums.edu
Section II: Advisor (if submitting student application)
Your advisor: Dr. Evornia Kincaid
Department: Elementary and Early Childhood Education
Address: Jackson State University P. O. Box 18380, SEB Suite #320
City, State, Zip Code: Jackson, MS 39217 - 0780
Telephone Number: 601 - 879 - 0442
JSU Email Address: evornia.kincaid@jsums.edu

Part II: Project Information

You are being asked to take part in a research study to determine the perceptions of Chinese parents about their children's formal school readiness in five domains and to examine their involvement in their children's preparation for kindergarten guided by their belief. The goal of the research project is to probe into the attitudes and motivations of Chinese parents and their practices to prepare children ready for kindergarten in a southern city of the U. S. And a thorough understanding of these can afford caregivers, parents, educators, and policy makers with insight concerning how early parenting contributes to young children's successful entry into kindergarten.

METHODS AND PROCEDURES:

The entire procedure should take approximately 60 minutes. If you agree to take part, you will be asked to participate in a one-time voluntary, in-person interview.

You will first be asked several questions about personal and background information such as your age, race, education level, etc. The interview will be recorded and transcribed by the researcher. The transcripts will then be analyzed by the researcher as well as several reviewers, who will only identify the transcripts by the code number. The records and transcripts will be stored in a locked cabinet in the researcher's home, and all records and hard copies will be destroyed three years after the end of the study. The interview data analysis process delineated by Kavale and Seidman was used by the researcher and guidance from Cresswell was also sought.

You will be given an explanation about the research subject and be asked to answer several questions based on the information you are given. Finally, you will be asked to complete two brief self-report forms. You may ask questions at any time during the study and you are free to contact my advisor or me if you have any questions about the research project.

RISKS AND DISCOMFORTS:

We expect no risks or discomfort for people in this study. However, it is possible that you may feel somewhat uneasy answering the questions involved.

BENEFITS:

The information obtained in this study may not directly benefit you. However, the results may provide needed information about Chinese parents' perceptions and involvement in school readiness that could be passed on to teachers and administrators. And this research will be beneficial to other early learning programs and policymakers looking to fund different programs by providing valuable information on improving school readiness practices.

CONFIDENTIALITY OF RECORDS:

All information obtained during this study is private. That is, we protect the privacy of people by withholding their names and other personal information from all persons not connected to this study. Each person will be identified using a code number rather than your name. The raw data shall be retained for 3 years, and all records relating to this research shall be retained for 3 years after completion of the research. All records shall be accessible for inspection and copying by authorized representatives of the Institutional Review Board at reasonable times and in a reasonable manner. Information will be stored in the most secure manner for 3 years as required by federal law. Although the information in this study is private, security of the data can only be promised within the boundaries of the university and researcher or faculty advisor. Confidentiality will be broken if the information obtained reveals that you intend to harm yourself or another person.

VOLUNTARY PARTICIPATION:

Taking part in this study is completely voluntary. You may refuse to answer any specific question. Participants may withdraw at any time without penalty or prejudice.

PARTICIPATION CONSENT:

I have had the purposes and procedures of this study explained to me and have had the opportunity to ask

Appendices

questions. My signature shows my willingness to take part in the study under the conditions stated. This study has been reviewed by the Institutional Review Board of Jackson State University, which ensures that research projects involving human subjects follow federal regulations. Any questions or concerns about rights as a research participant should be directed to Vice President for Research and Federal Relations, Jackson State University, P. O. Box 17057, Jackson, Mississippi, 39217, or (601) 979-2931.

_____ _____
     Participant Signature   Date

_____ _____
     Investigator Signature   Date

Appendix C: Interview Questions and Prompts

1. Could you please tell me something about your educational experience?

2. Could you please tell me some information about your children?

3. What kind of role are you in preparing your children for kindergarten?

4. What kind of education do your children receive before kindergarten, pre-school or home education? Why?

5. From your point of view, will/are your children be well prepared in kindergarten?

6. What factors contributed to your children's school readiness? Why are these factors important?

7. What practices do you employ to help your children get ready for kindergarten in physical well-being and motor development?

8. What practices do you employ to help your children get ready for kindergarten in social and emotional development?

9. What practices do you employ to help your children get ready for kindergarten in approaches toward learning?

10. What practices do you employ to help your children get

ready for kindergarten in language development?

11. What practices do you employ to help your children get ready for kindergarten in cognition and general knowledge?

12. Have you ever been confronted with any barriers in preparing your children ready for kindergarten in these five domains? What strategies will/do you employ in dealing with these barriers?

13. Have you ever changed your mind during the process of preparing your children for kindergarten? Why?

14. When you are engaged in your children's school readiness, what determined your strategies and practices?

15. Are these strategies and practices effective during your children's entry into kindergarten?

16. Is there anything that you would like to share with me that I did not ask?

Prompts Used During Interview:

What do you mean by ...?

Tell me more about ...

Could you explain a little more about ... (idea mentioned)?

Repetition or restatement of phrase.

Physical Prompts Used:

Lean forward.

Nod head.

Use encouraging body language.

Appendix D: Healing Children's Trauma after Hurricane Katrina

Introduction

Hurricane Katrina in August 2005 was responsible for devastation in southeastern Louisiana, southern Mississippi, and southwestern Alabama. This event also resulted in a storm surge along the coasts of Louisiana and Mississippi leading to widespread destruction. The storm surge overtopped and breached levees in the New Orleans metropolitan area including the eastern suburbs (National Hurricane Center, 2008). It was reported that more than 500,000 residents of Mississippi and Louisiana were evacuated during and after Hurricane Katrina, and more than 100,000 people were housed in temporary shelters in the country (Harvard Medical School, 2005). Many families lost their shelters and lived in poverty, which had negative effects on their young children's psychological development.

Many survivors from this event have been shown to have after-effects of that traumatic event through today (LaJoie, Sprang, & McKinney, 2010; Weems et al.,

2010). Hurricane Katrina resulted in high levels of stress, increased risk of psychological disorders (Osofsky, Kronenberg, & Tonya, 2010). Hurricane Katrina, like other natural disasters, has been reported to exhibit significant correlations with the prevalence of Post Traumatic Stress Disorder (PTSD) diagnoses in young children(Whaley, 2009). A large number of young children experienced increased sleep problems, nightmares, childhood fears, anger, sadness, withdrawal, behavioral difficulties, and general emotional stress. Some scholars argued that children were more susceptible to PTSD symptoms than the adult population (Fan, Zhang, Yang, Mo, and Liu, 2011). Many young children have been diagnosed with PTSD as a direct effect of Hurricane Katrina with need for special mental health care (Silverman, Allen, & Ortiz, 2010).

In order to heal these young children's psychological problems, many researchers pay more attention to parents, counselors, and young children. This event had and will continue to show a powerful effect on mental health of young children since the hurricane wrought by the storm was one of the worst natural disasters in American history. However, researches indicate that some young children are severely impaired by exposure to trauma whereas some others cope with trauma more effectively. It is necessary to identify the factors that affect young children's mental functioning in reaction to severe trauma, especially moderating their anxiety and PTSD symptoms. To have a better parent-children relationship and a better counselor-children relationship is beneficial to the healing of young children's PTSD symptoms.

Healing Children's Trauma from Counselors' Perspective

After Hurricane Katrina, some young children chose to leave the district and attend new schools while some others came back to the reopened schools. In this way, the role of professional school counselors exhibits a major influence on not only improving academic achievements but also on helping young children adjust to new environment and recover from the trauma. The professional school counselors could be called on to intervene in this event. This counseling could be individual or in groups, involving consulting with faculty, parents, and young children (Riley & McDaniel, 2000). Instant and solid support from the counselors could be effective for children's recovery. And their support can be helpful to community healing. They are also expected to offer counseling for the children and coordination of services both in school and in community (Smaby & Peterson, 1990). During and after the event, the weight of assisting the displaced children to heal and adjust was falling on the shoulders of professional school counselors. "School counselors are the only school personnel who are trained in both education and mental health. Because of this, they are uniquely qualified to collaborate with teachers and administrators to provide training as well as to identify and address hurricane-related problems among the young children"(*Katrina's Displaced Children*, 2005).

In spite of the findings of Hebert and Ballard(2007), that professional school counselors were among the very first groups to encounter and to help young children to recover from Hurricane Katrina's devastation, they were impacted by more than homeless, poverty-stricken surviving children on the brink of having PTSD. In addition, they were confronted with a population of approximately 90% African Americans (Moye, 2007). These Black and low-income children's sudden move into foreign social and educational settings could pose severe challenges to their transition and adjustment(Morris, 2006). Many poor Blacks were from low-performing schools with problems like high dropout rates, low test scores, unmotivated teachers, and no enough basic social welfare necessities.

According to diverse needs of different populations, the counselors could receive self-evaluation as the avenue to being more effective when having cross-cultural interpersonal interactions. The evacuee children were protected by the Mckinney-Vento Homeless Assistance Act which requires schools to help homeless children, involving those who have lost their homes because of a natural disaster (*Katrina's Displaced Children*, 2005). When these evacuee children came to the school, the counselors were required to help them to become stable even with shortage of counselor personnel. The Mailman School of Public Health, Columbia University announced that at least 46,600 children along the Gulf Coast were still haunted by Hurricane Katrina. So the task of the counselors was tough and long-term. These counselors found out that some children showed strong determination and spirit while some others experienced frustrated sense after interactions with these children.

When it comes to the children strengths that counselors perceive in Black Katrina evacuee children, the word resilience was the most frequently used one by the counselors. The word resilience means that the children possess the ability to bounce back to a sense of normality after a traumatic event. Some young children went through a great disaster and uprooted from their homes, but continued their day and were willing to adjust to another school or neighborhood community. And they showed the ability to use humor and a very strong sense of socialization to become survivors instead of victims. During their daily life, they began to make new friends, to have a more positive future, and to have hope. The fact was that many of the Black children after Hurricane Katrina were behind, but they did not lose their desire to stay in school and they were willing to work hard to succeed. They found out their learning potential and struggled to reach the standards for them even though that was not easy at the very beginning. And these young children in terms of resiliency were tightly related with the families whose adult members were looking for work, having gratefulness for any help, and possessing determination to make the transition to the new life.

Undoubtedly, the knowledge and skills of the counselors helped them to show their responsive services to the young children. They helped these children to remember how strong they truly were and that they could go through most anything. It was important not to treat the children as abnormal groups. Instead, they helped them to have some sense of normalcy, encouraged their Katrina children and reminded them of what they still have, what they have survived.

On contrary, trauma symptoms appeared in young children after this event. Young children seemed to be particularly at risk for the appearance of problems in many realms after trauma, including affect regulation, self-esteem, academic functioning, interpersonal relationships, and mood instability. Cohen et al. (2006) articulated that these problems fall within the category of complex PTSD. According to LaGreca et al. (2002), about 30% to 50% of young children affected by hurricanes are inclined to develop moderate to severe symptoms of PTSD. Young children impacted by this event were reported with high levels of stress. Osofsky et al. (2009) found that after this event factors such as displacement, parental unemployment, and home damage were tightly connected with PTSD, especially symptoms such as hyper-arousal and re-experiencing events.

Wells(2006) suggests that cases of acute stress reactions were found to be fewer than expected in that young children might be more able to alter and adapt when supplied with basic needs and nurturance. These children also tended to keep with primary care-givers instead of having additional stressors of separation anxiety.

Gender seemed to be a factor of how well children handle adversity. There was a study indicating that female young children tended to have PTSD symptoms following a major trauma. Female young children whose homes were flooded were more prone to severe PTSD symptoms. This finding of increased PTSD among female children was consistent with other studies and might be indicative of how children of different genders handle stress.

When confronted with the children with PTSD symptoms, the counselors could focus on personal counseling rather than only on academic counseling, specifically with young children. And empathy was another theme used commonly by the counselors, and the spectrum of empathy ranged from little empathy like telling children that Katrina stories will not work here to increased empathy like using the word "compassion" when delivering counseling services to young children post-Katrina. In addition, work responsibilities emerged when it came to the counseling work. The work responsibilities of these counselors changed after the hurricane with a major responsibility of implementing a comprehensive counseling program of academic, personal/social services before the hurricane and a focused responsibility of providing personal counseling services after the hurricane.

Besides, feeling reactions expressed by the counselors varied widely when faced with their work-related responsibilities after the hurricane. Positive responses such as "pleased, empowered, and validated" were expressed while negative responses like "angry, frustrated, overwhelmed, deceived, and upset" were expressed. Some served young children sharing similar experiences related to the natural disaster. On the other hand, some experienced frustration in work because the school system was in chaos with no functional plan or focus to improve the counseling situation and they could not be allowed to provide needed counseling services to the young children. As to the counselors, self-care was an ethical mandate and it was necessary for them to establish and maintain a professional perspective. The counselors tried a number of ways to maintain their attention to self-care, including going to the movies and library, taking small vacations, reading, going to church, being obsessed with music, taking self-talk and conversation with family members and friends, and so on.

Furthermore, many counselors experienced more tragic trauma and interacted on a daily basis with young children with similar traumatic events. So the counseling is a parallel process with two-fold counseling, healing the children and themselves. Some emerged with positive attitudes while some other counselors reacted with negative or debilitating effect. How the counselors coped with life and work after the hurricane had little to do with the magnitude of their traumas or losses. And it did not appear to depend on whether they had attended crisis training. It was that whether they engaged in self-care related to the circumstance they were faced with seemed to be directly connected to their emotional states as they performed their work after Katrina and to whether they were able to empathize with their traumatized young children clients. The exercise of self-care strategies positively affected their job performance for the counselors after Katrina. A parallel process appeared that connected the exercise of self-care strategies with positive emotional reactions to job responsibilities after the hurricane that mainly focused on personal counseling and empathy with young children.

It could be concluded that the counselors ought to establish a functional balance between caring for young children clients and caring for themselves so that they could effectively deal with the psychological problems of the young children post-Katrina.

Healing Children's Trauma from Parents' Perspective

Throughout the child anxiety literature, it was obvious

that parental anxiety was one of the most frequent risk factors for the emergence of child anxiety. Repeatedly, parental anxiety has been connected with child anxiety symptoms (Hudson & Rapee, 2002; Moore, Whaley, & Sigman, 2004). It was reported that children whose parents had more mental health problems were inclined to exhibit PTSD symptoms and anxiety. Parental anxiety pre-Katrina was expected to moderate the linkage between young children pre-Katrina anxiety and young children post-Katrina anxiety. It was believed that one of the major sources of social support for young children was the parent-child attachment relationship. Sandler's (2001) fourth need characterized social support as frequent, stable, positive interactions, and communication or bond with a significant person.

According to theories, the social support definition was almost the same as attachment. People with strong social support were more able to cope more effectively with traumas than those without strong social support. Availability of such supportive social relationships after the trauma regularly appeared as a significant predictor of recovery. As was described by Vernberg and Varela (2001), children, especially young children, depended upon their parents for protection and security. After a trauma, children's need for protection increased. It was imperative to have caretakers who maintained or re-established a sense of security and safety within the parent-child relationship after a natural disaster. Children with secure attachments might have more access to having limited PTSD symptoms; nevertheless, children with a history of poor attachments might become most vulnerable for any trauma. Specifically, children's psychopathology after the event was linked to lower subsequent self-esteem and more psychopathology in families if without supportive communication. Young children attachment belief to their parents before this hurricane tended to moderate the association between young children pre-Katrina anxiety and young children post-Katrina anxiety.

Parental attachment beliefs were conceptualized on two dimensions of interpersonal attachment-based cognitive styles(Bartholomew, 1990). The first one was called the Model of Self and characterized as a continuum of rejection from no fear and anxiety of rejection to intense anxiety and fear of rejection. The second one was called the Model of Others and had its range from interpersonal trust to intense interpersonal distrust, discomfort with interpersonal closeness, and avoidance of others.

Parental attachment beliefs were found to be one of the moderators of young children reactions to disasters. For instance, adults who had anxious attachments tended to hold negative perspectives about themselves or others regarding interpersonal relationships. These negative perspectives and behaviors might directly or indirectly influence their young children. When confronted with a trauma, like Hurricane Katrina, the inability for parents to effectively support their young children could become very detrimental to young children recovery from a disaster. Parental attachment beliefs before this event were expected to moderate the linkage between young children pre-Katrina anxiety and young children post-Katrina anxiety.

Parenting behaviors, especially rejection, psychological control, were proved to be significant predictors of young child anxiety. Rejecting parenting behaviors were featured by shortage of interactional warmth, acceptance of young children's feelings, active listening, praising, and behavioral and emotional involvement in young children's life and activities (Maccoby, 1983). Parenting behaviors like showing no acceptance of their young children's expressions of negative effect were detrimental to promotion of young children's emotion regulation because they always criticized and minimized their young children's feelings.

Psychologically controlling parenting behaviors involved inducing guilt, withdrawing love, disappointment and shaming by parents, instilling anxiety, infantilizing children, encouraging psychological and emotional dependence on the parent, and restricting children to the psychological world of parent (Barber & Harmon, 2001). It was supported that potentially negative or harmful parenting behaviors could hinder parents' ability to offer an effective social support system to their young children in reaction to disasters, like Hurricane Katrina. As a result, young children with low anxiety might have parents with secure attachment beliefs, low anxiety, and proper levels of parental acceptance and control before Katrina and they should have lower levels of anxiety after Katrina. Specifically, the parents with secure attachment beliefs, low anxiety, and proper levels of acceptance and control could afford adequate and effective levels of support for their young children. In other words, lower levels of parental anxiety, young children's insecure attachment beliefs, parental avoidant attachment beliefs, and controlling and rejecting parenting behaviors would be a beneficial factor for parents to successfully help their young children cope with the aftermath of Hurricane Katrina in a positive and warm way.

In contrast, young children with more anxiety together with parental anxiety, insecure beliefs, rejecting parenting behaviors, and improper levels of parental control before the event could be more likely to react to Hurricane Katrina with higher levels of anxiety. And parents with anxiety, rejecting parenting behaviors, insecure attachment beliefs, and improper control levels would become a negative source of support system for the young children faced with disasters.

Very strong family bonds assisted the Katrina young children to transit to their new environment. Closeness of the family motivated them to be resilient in making the best of their situation. When the adult members of the families were looking for work, grateful for any help, and determined to make transition to a new life, the term of resiliency was most used in these families. And the young children of these families were inclined to have a positive attitude both in school and in family. Mostly, the families only wanted what was best for their young children and they were receptive to any available help. Local churches adopted families and supplied a lot of support.

There were a diversified group of families. Some families were stable, concerned about their young children, and eager to return to a sense of normalcy. However, some other families were seemingly resentful to get involved with their young children's academic achievement and psychological development. Family cohesiveness was the strength and this term was used to involve the adult members of the families to the school work and help the young children to achieve success in school. Accordingly, the counselors could directly interact with the parents to enable them to have a stable psychological situation and return to normal life quickly so that their young children could hold a positive pace in the face with the disaster. In order to retain psychological resilience in disasters, the role of parents in young children was primary to help the young children to have positive changes after the hurricane. There were five major characteristics of resilience, including self-reliance, meaning, equanimity, perseverance, and existential aloneness. Specifically, self-reliance means a belief in oneself and one's capabilities, meaning the realization that life has a purpose and the valuation of one's contributions, equanimity a balanced view of one's life and experiences helping moderate extreme reactions to disasters, perseverance the act of persistence in spite of disasters, and existential aloneness the realization that everyone's life path is unique.

Psychological resilience in young survivors of Hurricane Katrina was essential to their well-being in that disastrous event resulted in psychological stress in anyone that experienced the event. In order to foster and maintain resilience, the young survivors of this event might be assisted by their parents to use some or all of Polk's proposed patterns of resilience, including dispositional, relational, situational, and philosophical. Dispositional pattern means psychosocial and physical attributes, relational pattern roles and relationships that affect resilience, situational pattern manifested as cognitive appraisal, problem-solving, and an ability to take steps during disasters, and philosophical pattern as the survivor's personal beliefs. Hence, psychological resilience of the young survivors was crucial to promote recovery after the event. The tight family cohesiveness and care from parents would play an important role in the recovery of young children after Hurricane Katrina.

Conclusion

To conclude, the devastating hurricane has exerted negative effects on young children's mental health. In order to lessen or eliminate the negative reactions of the young children to the hurricane, in particular fears and levels of anxiety, the young children could turn to the professional school counselors or their parents for help. The counselors could use their gained knowledge in responsive services with the young children. And the school counselors could be trained on regarding the children as part of a greater family system and to increase their counseling professionalism. And the counselors themselves should attach more importance to the issue of self-care in order to retain a balance between their work and lives. In addition, family cohesiveness was one of the greatest strengths for the young children, so the challenge of the parents was how to assist their young children to go through the stage of psychological healing. The parents could focus on both the physical and psychological needs of the young children and highlight what their young children really need.

References

Barber, B. K., & Harmon, E. L. (2001). Violating the self: Parental psychological control of children and adolescents. In B. K. Barber (Ed.), *Intrusive parenting: How psychological control affects children and adolescents* (pp. 125 - 159). Washington, DC: American Psychological Association.

Bartholomew, K. (1990). Attachment styles among young adults: A test of a four-category model. *Journal of Personality and Social Psychology*, 61, 226–244.

Cohen, J., Mannarina, A., & Deblinger, E. (1996). *Treating trauma and traumatic grief in children and adolescents*. New York: Guilford Press.

Fan, F., Zhang, Y., Yang, Y., Mo, L., & Liu, X. (2011). Symptoms of Posttraumatic Stress Disorder, Depression, and Anxiety among adolescents following the 2008 Wenchuan Earthquake in China. *Journal of Trauma Stress*, 24, 44–53. doi:10.1002/jts.20599

Harvard Medical School. (2005). *Hurricane Katrina advisory group*. Retrieved April 21, 2008, from the Harvard Medical School Web site: http://www.huricanekatrina.med.harvard.edu/presentations.php

Hebert, B., & Ballard, M. (2007). Children and trauma: A post-Katrina and Rita Response. *Professional School Counseling*, 11, 140–144.

Hudson, J., & Rapee, R. (2002). Parent-child interactions in clinically anxious children and their siblings. *Journal of Clinical Child and Adolescent Psychology*, 31, 548–555.

Katrina's Displaced School Children: Hearing before the Subcommittee on Education and Early Childhood Development of the Committee on Health, Education, Labor and Pensions, U.S. Senate, 109th Congress, 1st Sess., 16(2005)(testimony of Christopher Dodd).

La Greca, A., Prinstein, M., Vernberg, E., and Roberts, M. (2002). Children and disasters: Future directions for research and public policy Hurricanes and Earthquakes. In La Grecca, A., Silverman, W., Vernberg, E., & Roberts, M. (Eds.), *Helping children cope with disasters and terrorism.* Washington, DC: American Psychological Association.

LaJoie, A., Sprang, G., & McKinney, W. (2010). Long-term effects of Hurricane Katrina on the psychological well-being of evacuees. *Disasters,* 34(4), 1031–1044. doi:10.1111/j.14677717.2010.01181.x

Maccoby, E. E. & Martin, J. A. (1983). Socialization in the context of the family: Parent-child interaction. In M. Hetherington (Ed.), *Handbook of child psychology: Vol. 4. Socialization, personality, and social development.* (pp. 1–101). New York: Wiley.

Moore, P. S., Whaley, S. E., & Sigman, M. (2004). Interactions between mothers and children: Impact of maternal and child anxiety. *Journal of Abnormal Psychology,* 113, 471–476.

Morris, J. E. (2008). Out of New Orleans: Race, class, and researching the Katrina Diaspora. *Urban Education* 2008, 43. Retrieved June 1, 2008 from http://uex.sagepub.com.

Moye, L. A. (2007). *Face to face with Katrina survivors: A first responder's tribute.* Greensboro, NC: Open Hand Publishing, LLC.

National Hurricane Center. (2008). Hurricane preparedness: Hurricane history. Retrieved September 14, 2008, from the National Hurricane Center Web site: http://www.nhc.noaa.gov/HAW2/english/history.shtml#katrina

Osofsky, J. D., Osofsky, H. J., Kronenberg, M. H, Tonya, C. (2010). The aftermath of Hurricane Katrina: Mental health considerations and lessons learned. Washington, DC, US: *American Psychological Association*, 241 – 263.

Riley, P. L., & McDaniel, J. (2000). School violence prevention, intervention, and crisis response. *Professional School Counseling*, 4, 120 – 125.

Sandler, I. (2001). Quality and Ecology of Adversity as Common Mechanisms of Risk and Resilience. *American Journal of Community Psychology*, 29, 19 – 61.

Silverman, W. K., Allen, A., & Ortiz, C. D. (2010). Lessons learned from Hurricane Katrina and other devastating hurricanes: Steps necessary for adequate preparedness, response and intervention. *American Psychological Association*, 289 – 231.

Smaby, M. H. & Peterson, T. L. (1990). School-based community intervention: The school counselor as lead consultant for suicide. *School Counselor*, 37, 370 – 378.

Vernberg, E. M., & Varela, R. E. (2001). Post-traumatic stress disorder: A developmental perspective. In M. W. Vasey, & M. R. Dadds(Eds.), *The developmental psychopathology of disaster* (pp. 386 – 406). New York: Oxford University Press.

Weems, C. f., Taylor, L. K., Cannon, M. F., Marino, R. C., Romano, D. M., Scott, B. G., Perry, A. M., & Triplett, V. (2010). Post-traumatic stress, context, and the lingering effects of the Hurricane Katrina disaster among ethnic minority youth. *Journal of Abnormal Child Psychology,* 38(1), 49–56. DOI: 10.1007/s10802-009-9352-y.

Wells, M. (2006). Psychotherapy for families in the aftermath of disaster. *Journal of Clinical Psychology,* 62(8), 1017–1027.

Whaley, A. L. (2009). Trauma among survivors of Hurricane Katrina: Considerations and Recommendations for Mental Health Care. *Journal of Loss & Trauma,* 14(6), 459–476. DOI:10.1080/15325020902925480

Appendix E: Dissertation Critique

The dissertation selected was *Teachers' Perceptions of Leadership in Young Children* written by Deborah Lee Fox from University of New Orleans in 2012.

1. Introduction

In the introduction of the dissertation, the author clearly stated the purpose of the research was to explore how early childhood classroom teachers recognize leadership and how they projected they might influence leadership behaviors in young children, especially aged 4 through 6 years. The study was to mainly stress teacher recognition of child leadership behaviors and find the approaches to effect child leadership in classroom scenarios. The background information provided insight on issues associated with child leadership and its linkage to teachers' perceptions. Owing to the fact that there was a scarcity of child leadership information in the literature and the extensive researches of child leadership were also far from enough(Lee, Recchia, & Shin, 2005), the investigation conducted by the author can fill a void, especially within the early childhood settings.

Furthermore, it was suggested from the literature that the teachers might have difficulty in identifying the emerging characteristics of child leadership, thus they could not indicate how to encourage or discourage the behaviors of the children in class. According to the author's display, the research was worth investigating in that it can contribute to both policy and practice. For the aspect of policy, early childhood curriculum developers and directors might realize the importance to establish more child-directed activities. And for that of practice, the study allowed the teachers to recognize the leadership behaviors and support them so that this principal attribute could become a beneficial factor in children's future career. So, the numerous references the researcher cited in the introduction led the readers to be convinced that the arguments were reasonable and worthwhile.

Additionally, the issue discussed in the research was originated from the author's personal and professional experiences with her triple roles as a student, parent, and teacher, who actively struggled to promote the understanding of socio-emotional needs of children which might involve leadership behaviors(Fox, 2012). Also, the final section included a brief and explicit explanation of a large number of terms which might be unacquainted with the readers, including Developmentally Appropriate Practice, developmental domains, dispositions, gifted, NAEYC, and so on.

2. Review of the Literature

Chapter Two was the literature review, which was made up of several subtopics, involving an overall analysis of four key elements, the concept of leadership, child leadership characteristics and instruments to measure child leadership, the relevant research studies available, the ways in which teachers influence children's social skills. These points seemed to adequately outline a comprehensive approach to the identified area of study. On account of large quantities of definitions and theories about adult leadership, no consensus about the understanding of leadership existed(Burns, 1978; Schulz, 2001). The author mainly introduced four theories most commonly related to adult leadership in the literature, including trait, behavioral pattern or style, situational pattern or contingency, and transactional and transformational theories of leadership. However, the prior researches about child leadership were small in quantity, and so were those in how leadership manifests in classroom. Researchers like Parten(1932), Adcock and Segal(1983), Mullarkey(2005) observed leadership among children. Bisland (2004), Karnes and Bean(1996), Lee et al.(2005) provided specific suggestions to assist teachers promote leadership skills in the classroom.

Moreover, an overall review of summary of characteristics

of child leadership and current formal and informal instruments to measure leadership in children has been depicted. And of the researcher-designed instruments mentioned, the Least Preferred Playmate Scale differed from the others and researchers evaluated children's leadership styles rather than characteristics(Fiedler et al., 1976). Among the mentioned 26 studies, the author classified them into five types, teachers nominated, classified, or described student leader, studies in which researchers nominated the student leaders, studies in which researchers used test data and observations, studies in which students evaluated peers using sociograms, peer rating, or self-reporting, and studies in which parents nominated or described leaders. Nevertheless, the author also put forward her disagreement with some of the studies in that these studies may have simply looked for children who demonstrated leadership traits and might not have looked at leadership emerging from situations and the results of these studies may not be generalized to other populations. And the majority of the studies reviewed were not based on teachers to identify leaders. As a result, the study that the author has completed, to a great extent, was researchable and necessary.

3. Methodology

Chapter Three was methodology, in which qualitative

and quantitative methods were both validated in order to increase the reliability of the study. The author described the research method thoroughly, starting by pointing out the respective data collection to answer the three research questions. The research design employed in the study was the Concurrent Triangulation Design, which can collect both quantitative and qualitative data simultaneously and equally (Creswell and Plano Clark, 2007). The survey instrument was the Recognizing Leadership in Children (RLIC) Survey, a commonly and efficiently used tool in figuring out leadership in children.

The methodology for data collection was clearly articulated and the collecting data procedure promoted the researcher's ability to investigate and answer the research questions. The preparation and design of the research, undoubtedly, was sufficient and cogitative. After receiving admission from IRB, the author asked the participants to answer the questions in each of the scenarios. The process of data collection was accomplished over a period of two and a half months.

In order to guarantee the reliability and content validity of the RLIC Survey, Kuder-Richardson procedures were used to determine the internal consistency of the scale with a value of 0.79 to meet the criteria of reliability. And the author got in touch with five experts to evaluate and provide feedback upon the content of the survey. Even though not all the experts afforded extensive evaluation and feedback, the scenarios and items involved have been modified, added or deleted to improve the RLIC Survey.

Abiding by the principles of generalization and representation, the samples were randomly selected teachers of early childhood grades in public, private, and parochial schools over the state of Louisiana with even ages distribution. In terms of data analysis methods, the author conducted the quantitative data analysis by means of IBM SPSS Statistics Version 19.0 and the qualitative analysis according to the book *Qualitative Data Analysis: An Expanded Sourcebook* (Miles and Huberman, 1994).

4. Results

Chapter Four provided the readers with the results of the study, which integrated quantitative and qualitative studies to respond to the three research questions related to the study. Upon the first question, the researcher obtained results of qualitative findings by means of interviews and surveys, presenting clear descriptions. In accordance with Table 9, the descriptors most supplied by teachers in written answers were listed from the most frequent one (Helpful) to the least one (Not bossy, follows rules, sought out by peers). Comparatively, 35% of the descriptors from the participants were involved in the most principal features of child leadership in the literature. Given the scenarios, the second question was addressed with both quantitative reports and qualitative findings.

After frequency analysis of correct answering percentages by IBM SPSS Version 19.0, another finding came into being that teachers recognized child leadership more often when it was obvious than they did in less obvious examples(Fox, 2012). To further discuss teachers' recognition of leadership in children, two sub-questions were proposed, including the correlations between years of experience and the number of correct responses and between reported training in child leadership and the number of correct figurations. As a result, the Pearson Product Correlation test released a result that both of the variables made no difference in the participants' identification of child leadership on the condition of different scenarios.

Next, qualitative findings regarding the third research question was put forward in the light of responses to the questions on the RLIC Survey. Similarly, descriptive statistics were utilized to run frequencies analysis. Data from this study confirmed the findings in the literature that suggested teachers encourage, discourage, and ignore child leadership(Maxcy, 1991; Mullarkey et al., 2005). It was exhibited that this study revealed how in-service teachers described, recognized, and might offer feedback to child leaders.

5. Discussion

Chapter Five was discussion, which informed the readers the discussion of the findings, limitations, delimitations, implications, recommendations for future research. There were altogether nine findings emerging from the analysis, which specifically replied to the three research questions. Teachers employed descriptors not only from the literature on child leadership, but from adult theories of leadership as well. Obvious scenarios saw easier recognition of child leadership and teachers were more sensitive to child leaders when classroom rules were violated and when the leaders took on a teacher's role. Contrarily, the scenarios were the most difficult to identify child leadership when children helped or volunteered and when children played in centers or at recess outside(Fox, 2012). In addition, the responses from teachers towards child leaders were multiple, from discouraging, ignoring, encouraging, and mixed comments, where discouragement was slightly more than encouragement. There was no significant distinction in the responses between RL and DNRL teachers, only with a tendency that RL teachers wrote more encouragements than DNRL ones.

The limitations of this study included the following four points, the participants' reluctance to respond honestly, the limitation of the RLIC Survey, no consensus in the definition of child leadership for the teachers to recognize, and lack of administrators. In terms of the delimitations, the participants were restricted to teachers in pre-kindergarten, kindergarten, or first grade at that time and located in the state of Louisiana. Even though the study had its limitations and delimitations, there still existed underlying implications and suggestions for future work. It was suggested that the teachers be aware that children aged 4 through 6 years are in the "initiative versus guilt" developmental stage (Erikson, 1963) and they exert influences over children (Adcock & Segal, 1983; Bronfenbrenner, 1979; Maxcy, 1991). It was of great vitality for the teachers to realize the importance to encourage young children's emerging leadership. Additionally, due to the fact that the study was an exploratory research on the basis of the previous studies, teacher recognition and responses regarding the gender of the child could turn to be the research focus in the future work. And the future extending researches might also shed light on cultural diversity, teachers' certification, recognition rates of the gifted, and so on. Nevertheless, the organization of delivering research results, findings, and discussion was somewhat confusing, which could be better managed to clearly demonstrate the results.

6. Synthesis

Admittedly, this dissertation contributed much to my

project in that it provided an overall literature review of the child leadership and the impacts from the teachers on child leadership. The deficiency of child leadership in literature allows my project to add to the void and is constantly reminding me of the great significance to conduct a research on child leadership. It is assumed that the stress on child leadership development could be a beneficiary factor in one's future career life. Different from this study, my project is mainly a concern about the correlation between maternal attitudes and Chinese American children's leadership development, with diverse perspective and more confined population. Because the limitations and problems of this study have been explicitly explained, the considerations with regard to my project may attach importance to random selection of the participants, logical interpretation of the findings, the careful management of the biased data, and the clear allocation of the structure of the dissertation in order to boost the reliability and validity of my project.

References

Adcock, D., & Segal, M. (1983). *Making Friends: Ways of encouraging social development in young children*. Englewood Cliffs, NJ: Prentice-Hall.

Bisland, A. (2004). Developing leadership skills in young gifted students. *Gifted Child Today,* 27(1), 24 – 27.

Bronfenbrenner, U. (1979). *The ecology of human development: Experiments by nature and design*. Cambridge, MA: Harvard University Press.

Burns, J. M. (1978). *Leadership*. New York, NY: Harper & Row.

Creswell, J. W., & Plano Clark, V. L. (2007). *Designing and conducting mixed methods research*. Thousand Oaks, CA: Sage.

Erikson, E. (1963). *Childhood and society*. New York, NY: W. W. Norton.

Fiedler, F., Chemers, M., & Maher, L. (1976). *Improving leadership effectiveness: The leader match concept*. New York, NY: John Wiley & Sons.

Fox, D. L. (2012). *Teachers' perceptions of leadership in young children* (Doctoral dissertation). Retrieved from http://ecnhts-proxy.jsums.edu:2184/pqdtglobal/docview/1315001762/DADA87EC42174702PQ/1?accountid=11661

Karnes, F., & Bean, S. (1996). Leadership and the gifted. *Focus on Exceptional Children, 29*(1), 1–12.

Lee, S. Y., Recchia, S., & Shin, M. S. (2005). "Not the same kind of leaders": Four young children's unique ways of influencing others. *Journal of Research in Childhood Education, 20*(2), 132–148.

Maxcy, S. J. (1991). Leadership and the education of young children. In S. J. Maxcy, *Educational Leadership: A critical pragmatic perspective*. (pp. 95–109). Toronto,

Ontario: OISE.

Miles, M., & Huberman, A. (1994). *Qualitative data analysis: An expanded sourcebook.* (2nd ed.). Thousand Oaks, CA: Sage.

Mullarkey, L. S., Recchia, S. L., Lee, S. Y., Shin, M. S., & Lee, Y. J. (2005). Manipulative managers and devilish dictators: Teachers' perspectives on the dilemmas and challenges of classroom leadership. *Journal of Early Childhood Teacher Education,* 25, 123 - 129.

Parten, M. (1932). Social participation among pre-school children. *The Journal of Abnormal and Social Psychology,* 27(3), 243 - 269. doi: 10.1037/h0074524

Schulz, W. (2001). Changing definitions of leadership. In W. Schulz, *Leadership: An overview.* Retrieved from http://www.infinitefutures.com/essays/publichealth/leadershiphtml/

Appendix F: Lesson Plan

1. Lesson Plan

a. Subject
Reading: Literature

b. Grade Level
Second

c. Summary
The lesson is designed to help students explore the concepts of beginning, middle, ending and group characters by reading stories and mapping ideas in the concept-mapping software Gliffy. There is a growing literature examining the development of young children' ability to comprehend and interpret stories (e.g., Corriveau, Chen, & Harris, 2014; Corriveau, Kim, Schwalen, & Harris, 2009; Kendeou, Bohn-Gettler, White, & van den Broek, 2008; Trabasso & Wiley, 2005; Weisberg, Goodstein, Sobel, & Bloom, 2013), as well as the various factors that affect learning and generalization from stories (e.g., Chiong & DeLoache, 2012; Fazio & Marsh, 2008; Ganea, Canfield, Ghafari, & Chou, 2014). The Concept Development Model is used for

the students to gradually and accurately form the concepts. To start the teaching of the subject, the ASSURE model has been adopted to create lessons that validly unite the use of technology and media to guide children's learning experiences. The ASSURE model consists of six step-by-step stages, analyzing learners, stating standards and objectives, selecting strategies and resources, utilizing resources, requiring learner participation, and evaluating and revising.

d. Standards

Common Core State Standard Grade 2 #5: Describe the overall structure of a story, including describing how the beginning introduces the story and the ending concludes the action.

National Educational Technology Standards for Students (NETS-S) 2007 #1 and #2.

NCTE/IRA 3: Students apply a wide range of strategies to comprehend, interpret, evaluate, and appreciate texts.

e. Objectives/Learning Goals

Students will be able to identify beginnings, middles, and endings in some familiar stories.

Students will be able to make some generalizations of basic elements of story structure.

Students will be able to list the characters in the stories and group them.

Students will be able to employ a concept-mapping tool,

like Gliffy software, to express and explore their ideas.

f. Instructional Model

The Concept Development Model is adopted in this lesson. The model, an interactive, engaging instructional model, encourages learners to extend and improve their understanding of concepts via multiple cognitive processes. And students' inherited trait to long for new knowledge allows them to add new concepts into their existing conceptual frameworks. There are five steps (listing, grouping, labeling, regrouping, synthesizing) in the Concept Development Model, in which the inductive thinking tasks are embedded. This model promotes students to have critical-thinking skills, build content knowledge, and make use of their diverse backgrounds and prior knowledge.

g. Cognitive Process Dimension

In line with Bloom's taxonomy, there are altogether six categories in cognitive process dimension, including remembering, understanding, applying, analyzing, evaluating, and creating. It involves *remember* and *understand* categories in listing and grouping; it addresses *analyze* category in grouping and demonstrating.

h. Types of Knowledge

The knowledge learned in this lesson is conceptual

knowledge with sub-types as categories and structures and factual knowledge. For instance, understanding of story structure in the first and second objectives belongs to the knowledge of structure whereas grouping characters in the third objective conforms to the area of categories. And the knowledge of the use of Gliffy is part of factual knowledge.

2. Learning Context

a. General Rationale

Learning goals are not intended to boundary what students learn, but rather are designed to supply a minimum level of expected achievement. Serendipitous or incidental learning should be encouraged because learning takes different forms with different students. When planning lesson curriculums, the desired result of instruction is one of the most important parts. After setting goals of learning, the teacher will be better prepared to identify the best approaches and materials for instruction and determine what acceptable evidence of mastery is. Besides, the teacher could examine whether the students make progress toward the goal by means of assessment and instruction could be modified and interventions can occur during the student's learning. Furthermore, concise goals can keep the emphasis on the learning content and maximize teaching time. The completion of these objectives could facilitate the students to initiate and master their writing techniques.

b. Specific Rationale

Regarding the first and second objectives, beginning, middle, ending are defined as the three parts that make up a story. Identifying these three parts assists the students to comprehend how organization, sequence, and plot make a complete story. Furthermore, this technique could then be applied to the writing of the students.

In terms of the third objective, when the students master the ability to identify characters and group them into positive and negative groups, their tentative skill of conclusion and induction has been developed. In addition, the students could learn virtue from the positive characters and avoid imitating the evil behaviors of the negative characters.

Gliffy is a tool for students to have visual learning, which helps them to clarify their thoughts, organize and analyze information, integrate new knowledge, and think critically. Visual thinking and learning utilize graphical approached of working with ideas and expressing information. Many researchers suggest that visual learning is one of the very best ways of teaching students of early age how to think and how to learn.

c. Learner Characteristics

Diverse learners include students from racially, ethnically, culturally, and linguistically diverse families and communities of lower socioeconomic status, and students with disabilities. The growing diversity in class promotes the development and application of diverse teaching strategies designed to respond to each student as an individual. Economically disadvantaged children may have problems like delayed language acquisition, vision and hearing problem, poor nutrition. The bilingual learners need instructional contexts to improve their transfer of knowledge from the first language to the second. In the field of special education, the majority of children with disabilities are served in the general education classroom with support services. Nearly half of elementary students with disabilities were found to have a speech or language impairment.

Generally, children at this age usually have short attention spans, so activities of small pieces or steps with active physical movements work best. All new learning contains use of language. Both boys and girls tend to focus on the "doing of a project" instead of the completion of a project. And they turn to be concrete thinkers doing better in activities where they are doing and seeing things.

In addition, the students have a strong desire to feel accepted and approved by adults. They attain satisfaction from praise and encouragement of small successes. Besides, they enjoy working with plenty of adult attention. They begin to identify with a peer group and want to belong by spending more time with friends. As a result, in this lesson the teacher plans to design group work and expresses approval of students' work.

3. Methodology

a. Preparation

Before beginning this lesson, the students were asked to review the following stories.

Cinderella   *Snow White*
The Three Little Pigs   *The Frog Prince*

The prepared materials include:

Edited video of *Snow White*;

Colorful printouts of *Snow White*;

Some large print and highlighted printouts;

Masks of characters in *Snow White*;

Installation of Gliffy;

Two Gliffy files including the characters and beginnings and endings of the stories for students who might have difficulty in listing by themselves.

b. Procedures

Lead-in: (5 minutes)

The teacher asks students to review the stories listed last time. Then, an edited version of video of *Snow White* is played to help the students strengthen their memory of the story.

Listing: (5 minutes)

After watching the video, the teacher activates students to work in groups to discuss two questions, how this story begins

Appendices

and ends and what happens in the middle, and list all the characters in *Snow White*. This is a computer-based activity because the concept-mapping program Gliffy is used to assist them to list everything they remember from the story. Students could use fragments of ideas rather than complete sentences. For example, one of the groups lists some phrases "once upon a time, gentle and kind, ran deep into the woods, trick the princess, one bite of the apple, the spell was broken, returned to the kingdom, lived happily ever after", "Snow White, the Queen, Huntsman, the Seven Dwarfs, Prince Charming". This process is conducted on Gliffy, with which the students do their brainstorming. This program allows them to type these thought bubbles of information in different-shaped boxes. The teacher circulates among the students, observing their work and helping students in need. Meanwhile, the students can observe the work of their peers by taking turns to walk around the classroom.

Grouping: (5 minutes)

The teacher promotes the groups to consider whether they can put some ideas into one box. In this activity, the students use Gliffy to move the ideas into different groups on the computer screen and number these groups. The underlying intention of the grouping is to put ideas into beginning, middle, ending and put characters into positive and negative group. The teacher takes the responsibility to help the students group or facilitate appropriate groups.

For example, one of the groups has the following grouping:

Group 1: once upon a time, gentle and kind

Group 2: ran deep into the woods, trick the princess, one bite of the apple

Group 3: the spell was broken, returned to the kingdom, lived happily ever after

Group a: Snow White, Huntsman, the Seven Dwarfs, Prince Charming

Group b: the Queen

Labeling: (5 minutes)

With the help of the teacher, the students try to label each group. Gliffy is used to label groups. Additionally, they can differentiate the groups by labeling them and changing different shapes. In this step, the teacher circulates around the classroom and provides suggestions on correct labeling. For example, one of the groups gives the groups of story structure's elements the shape of square and characters triangle.

Beginning: once upon a time, gentle and kind

Middle: ran deep into the woods, trick the princess, one bite of the apple

Ending: the spell was broken, returned to the kingdom, lived happily ever after

Positive character: Snow White, Huntsman, the Seven Dwarfs, Prince Charming

Negative character: the Queen

Synthesizing: (5 minutes)

After labeling, the teacher and the students complete the generalization together. The teacher initiates the sentence "the basic elements of story structure include ...", followed by the answer from the students "beginning, middle, and ending". Apart from this, the teacher explains the differences between positive and negative characters and instructs students to learn from the positive characters.

Role-Play: (5 minutes)

After clearly and correctly grouping all the characters, it is time for the students to role play the characters. The whole class is divided into several groups and members of each group play the main roles in the story. These students wear the masks marked by the names of the characters and come out with a line "I am ...".

Evaluation and conclusion: (10 minutes)

The teacher chooses another familiar story *Cinderella* and asks all groups to talk about its beginning, middle, and ending. The teacher examines the points in the checklist. Then, each member of the groups represents one or more characters of *Cinderella*. Afterwards, the students representing positive characters raise their hands.

Finally, the teacher concludes the content and points out the missing parts in the evaluation step.

c. Plan for Differentiation

In spite of the fact that the standards should be met by all students, differentiation still occurs in class. For one thing, for those with high achieving gifts, they have already attained the understanding of story structure and categories of characters, so they might be challenged to extend the exploration of story structure and character categories. For instance, they might be asked to consider more complicated story structure and work independently or in groups to find out the definitions of heroes and heroines. When the teacher examines the discussion and performance of students, the teacher could add a term "climax" to demonstrate the most exciting moment in the story. And from grouping the characters, these students could find out the clue about the main characteristics of the most important figures in the story. The teacher could assist them to give a simple definition by means of Gliffy.

For the other thing, for those with mild disabilities in a "general education" classroom, they might have delayed speech or language acquisition. In order to meet specific needs of these students, it could be an effective way to modify various aspects of the classroom or instruction, like modification in environment, instructional materials, presentation, and evaluation. For example, the teachers could supply large print and highlighted handouts for students with visual problem, prepare high interest and low vocabulary books for students with delayed language acquisition, and present lecture note in advance.

d. Plans for Technology

Technology is assisting teachers to extend beyond linear, text-based learning and encourage students to learn best in other ways. It means that teachers can employ a versatile learning tool that could alter how to demonstrate concepts, assign projects and assess progress. The adoption of technology in class might have better simulations and models, allow multimedia to engage all the senses in learning, and lead to more efficient assessment. First, the video played in the lead-in activity helps students to capture the whole story with all their senses and the highlighted parts of beginning, middle, and ending stimulate students to think about the story structure. Second, the use of Gliffy is an aid for students to map a concept visually because when students list the main parts of a story structure and label them, these fragments of ideas could constitute the concept of a story structure's necessity.

e. Anticipation of Difficulty

Although it is expected that all the students should be engaged in activities and all the preparations are thorough and invulnerable, some unexpected disfunction might happen in the middle of the lesson. Firstly, when allocating the listing activity, some students might struggle generating their own lists. In this case, the teacher should create the listing file in advance to assist these students. Secondly, for the students with diverse cultural backgrounds or English second language learners, the teacher might repeat the instructions slowly and spend some time explaining the cultural background. Thirdly, if the computer or other technological tools break down, alternative materials have to be prepared. For instance, coloring handouts of story lines and large-sized pictures of characters should be printed out when the video cannot be released. And the teacher could make use of an alternative plan, like read-aloud activity in which the teacher mimics the voices of different characters and highlights beginning, middle, and ending by raising the volume or repeating the parts.

4. Assessment

a. Student Assessment

Formative assessments are used to check whether the students have grasped know-how in learning objectives. Assessment is essential to the development of quality instruction, whose ultimate question is whether students have grasped what they are supposed to learn. As a result, the assessment tasks will require students to demonstrate the behavior stated in the learning objectives.

For the first objective, the teacher chooses one of the familiar stories, such as *Cinderella*, and requires the students to talk about its beginning, middle, and ending.

For the second one, according to their performance in the generalization of basic elements of story structure, the teacher could evaluate whether they have attained the correct concept of story structure.

For the third one, the assessment material is still *Cinderella*, in which the students are asked to list the characters and group them into two categories, positive and negative.

For the final one, the teacher observes the use of Gliffy by the students and checks the final Gliffy files.

b. Lesson Assessment

In addition to student assessment, assessment of the design and implementation of the lesson is one of the indispensable parts, which may help the teacher to collect the feedback, determine the efficiency of the lesson, and revise strategies and resources. Despite the fact that lesson assessment may give rise to some apprehension, the resulting messages will supply with excellent feedback for addressing areas of needed improvement. This assessment could be conducted through discussions and interviews. During the lesson, the teacher could use debriefing activities and informal talks with the students in order to find out whether they think the activities and resources are worthwhile.

The assessment could involve four types of evaluation: self, student, peer, and administrator. For self-assessment, an audio or video recording of the teacher's instruction could encourage the teacher to listen to or view later on. For the students, they are willing to share ideas in a group or submit comments anonymously. For peers, the teacher could invite a colleague to sit in the back of the room and observe the instruction, after which he or she could provide feedback in an open-ended evaluation, like a blank sheet of paper. For administrators, they could be invited to observe the teaching and give some feedback.

c. Rationale

In terms of student assessment, the chosen assessment methods are age appropriate for Grade Two students because spoken English expression is more operable than abstract paper-and-pencil tasks. In addition, the assessments are linguistically appropriate, recognizing that to some extent all assessments methods are measures of language. Although the assessments are intended to measure whether students have grasped story structure and grouping of characters, the design of articulating the results is easily confounded by language proficiency, especially for children from home backgrounds with less exposure to English. Furthermore, the design of assessments is tailored to specific purposes with reliability, validity, and fairness. With regard to lesson assessments, the evaluation from four different groups could provide a full-scale feedback to the lesson efficiency. The teacher could take advantage of the experience from colleague and administrator and update the quality of the instruction. After the evaluation, if discrepancies between the intentions and what actually happen are large, the teacher could go back to the faulty part of the plan and modify it.

d. Assessment Plan and Tools

The first assessment task is a formative assessment. After group discussion, they will talk about their answers and the teacher is responsible for examining the points of beginning, middle, and ending in the checklist. If they get two points correctly, they basically grasp the structure of *Cinderella*.

After the first task, all the students are required to conclude the concept of basic elements of story structure with the guidance of the teacher. The teacher initiates the generalization like "Generally, the story structure has three main elements, that is", and the students complete the sentence like "beginning, middle, and ending". After examining their responses to the teacher's question, the teacher could find out the target students who have not constructed the right concept. These students might be required to review the content and answer the question again.

The second assessment task is to ask each member of the groups to represent one or more characters of *Cinderella*. Afterwards, the students representing positive characters could raise their hands. This is an alternative assessment.

To examine whether the students are able to use

Gliffy, the teacher observes their application through the whole lesson process. If they could sequence beginning, middle, and ending and graphing two groups of characters, positive and negative, the teacher could determine that they have mastered the usage of Gliffy.

References

Chiong, C., & DeLoache, J. S. (2012). Learning the ABC's: What kind of picture books facilitate young children's learning? *Journal of Early Childhood Literacy,* 13, 225 – 241. doi:10.1177/1468798411430091

Corriveau, K. H., Chen, E. E., & Harris, P. (2014). Judgments about fact and fiction by children from religious and non-religious backgrounds. *Cognitive Science.* Advance online publication. doi: 10.1111/cogs.12138

Corriveau, K. H., Kim, A. L., Schwalen, C. E., & Harris, P. (2009). Abraham Lincoln and Harry Potter: Children's differentiations between historical and fantasy characters. *Cognition,* 113, 213 – 225. doi: 10.1016/j. cognition. 2009.08.007

Fazio, L. K., & Marsh, E. J. (2008). Older, not younger, children learn more false facts from stories. *Cognition,* 106, 1081 – 1089. doi:10.1016/j.cognition.2007.04.012

Ganea, P. A., Canfield, C. F., Ghafari, K. S., & Chou, T. (2014). Do cavies talk? The effect of anthropomorphic picture books on children's knowledge about animals. *Frontiers in Psychology*. Advance online publication. doi: 10.3389/fpsyg.2014.00283

Kendeou, P., Bohn-Gettler, C., White, M. J., & van den Broek, P. (2008). Children's inference generation across different media. *Journal of Research in Reading*, 31, 259 – 272. doi:10.1111/j.1467-9817.2008.00370.x

Trabasso, T., & Wiley, J. (2005). Goal plans of action and inferences during comprehension of narratives. *Discourse Processes*, 29, 129 – 164. doi: 10.1080/0163853X.2005.9651677

Weisberg, D., Goodstein, J., Sobel, D. M., & Bloom, P. (2013). Young children are reality-prone when thinking about stories. *Journal of Cognition and Culture*, 13, 383 – 407. doi:10.1163/15685373-12342100

Appendix G: Enhancing Pre-K in Mississippi

Introduction

The core purpose of the P-20 is to establish a system beneficial for students through career pathways and their academics, including arts and communication, business, technology, engineering, health sciences, sciences, and so on. P-20 is placed into the school systems for all students to learn experiences and acquire academic skills so that they will enhance their education and attain employment credentials to have higher job opportunities through rigorous coursework. Nevertheless, Mississippi has the deficiency in the research to integrate the particular system into their curriculum designing.

Despite growing national interest in better aligning and extending the K-12 and post-secondary education systems, various states adopt different P-20 education systems when arranging the goals of different stages and focusing on transitions between stages. Even though neighboring states have made great strides in early childhood education,

Mississippi remains to fail in an attempt to prepare children for kindergarten or first grade. By means of comparing Mississippi's prekindergarten and other states', policy makers in Mississippi can learn from the leading states in early education and enhance young children's kindergarten readiness rates.

Pre-K in the State of Florida

In the year of 2004, the State of Florida initiated the Voluntary Prekindergarten Program, which provides all four-year-old children in Florida with free prekindergarten services regardless of their family income. The VPK program is intended to offer early learners opportunities to succeed in kindergarten and beyond and build a strong foundation for school. Parents can choose from a variety of educational settings and different program options, such as private childcare centers, public schools and specialized instructional services providers.

VPK Program Options

A school-year program offers 540 hours of instruction with class sizes no more than 20 children. A summer program involves 300 instructional hours with class sizes no larger than 12 students. Parents whose 4 - year-old children have special needs may choose the VPK Specialized

Instructional Services educational program, where certified or licensed professionals supply instruction in individual or small group settings. However, the option requires the child to own a current individual education project from a local school district. Children attending high-quality preschool do perform better when they get to kindergarten, and it makes an enormous difference for their later academic and career success. According to a research by the University of Chicago economist James J. Heckman, a Nobel laureate, he points to a 7-to-10-percent annual return rate on investment in high-quality preschool.

Florida's Voluntary Prekindergarten Specialized Instructional Services education program is an additional option for 4 year olds with disabilities outside the traditional VPK classroom setting. If a child has a current individual educational plan from a local school district that requires specialized instructional services, he or she can choose VPK SIS instead of traditional school year or summer programs. VPK specialized instructional services are offered in individual or small group settings with a certified or licensed professional trained to provide specific instruction. Students enrolled in VPK SIS may use services issued on their individual educational plans, such as applied behavior analysis, speech language pathology, occupational therapy, physical therapy, listening and spoken language instruction, and other specialized instructional services. Parents can select one or more services and choose from providers the Florida Department of Education has approved. Funding for each student is equivalent to traditional VPK, but based on the rates these specialists charge for their services. As a result, students in VPK SIS are likely to receive fewer hours of service than those in traditional VPK.

There are many merits of VPK. The most pivotal growth and development in the brain emerges around the age of five. The early years are the learning years. Children's ability to be attentive and to follow directions happens in the early years. Structured early learning promotes these abilities for later success both in school and in career. Pre-K prepares children to be ready for school. Children involved in high-quality early childhood education programs are inclined to acquire better language skills, score higher in school-readiness tests and develop better social skills and fewer behavioral problems. In addition, they are also better prepared for Kindergarten, especially in the realms of pre-reading, pre-math and social skills. Pre-K develops a love of learning in children. Pre-K improves what a child learns at home and instills a love of life-long learning.

The following charts (Chart 1, Chart 2, Chart 3) display data related to the VPK program and the VPK provider kindergarten readiness rates.

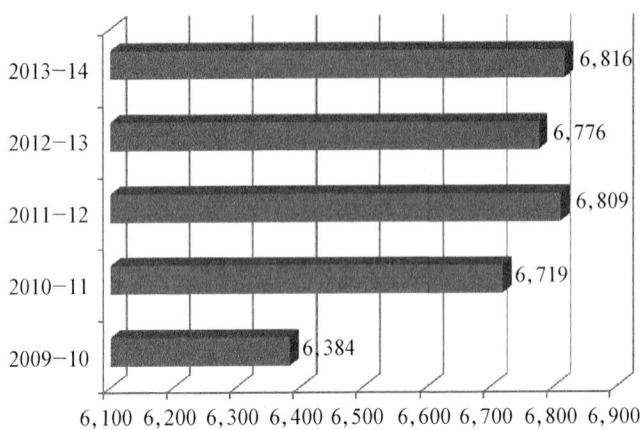

The chart comes from FLKRS_VPK_Accountability_Overview_11-07-14, p.4.

Chart 1　Number of VPK Programs by Year

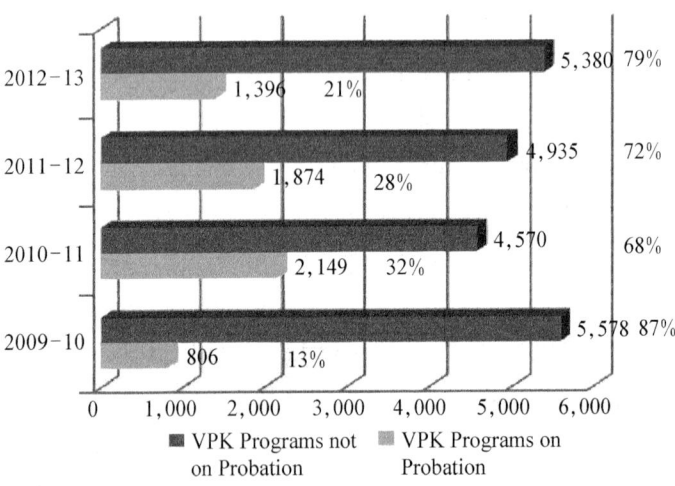

The chart comes from FLKRS_VPK_Accountability_Overview_11-07-14, p.5.

Chart 2　VPK Provider Readiness Rate Trends

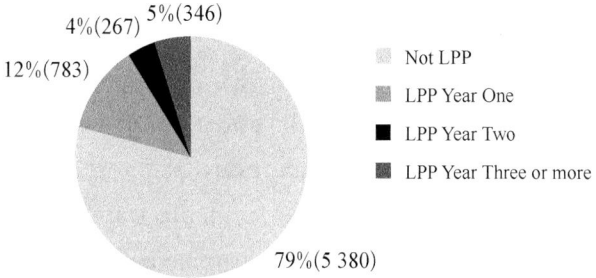

The chart comes from FLKRS_ VPK _ Accountability_ Overview_11 - 07 - 14, p.5.

Chart 3　VPK Providers Not Meeting the Minimum Readiness Rate(1,396)—Low Performing Providers(LPP) Status

Florida Kindergarten Readiness Screener(FLKRS)

Florida Kindergarten Readiness Screener(FLKRS) is employed to inform the kindergarten teachers instructional information about the children entering kindergarten. Legislation regulating uniform statewide kindergarten screening system for all public school kindergarten students came into effect in 1999 - 2000. Prior to FLKRS, districts screened kindergarten students applying individual, district-adopted measures. Section(s.) 1002.69(5), Florida Statutes (F. S.), implementing the Voluntary Prekindergarten (VPK) Education Program, regulates that the department shall require every school district to administer the statewide kindergarten screening upon each kindergarten student in the school district within the first 30 school days of each school year.

The screening collects information about children's overall development and addresses their readiness for kindergarten on the basis of performance standards used in VPK, currently the Florida Early Learning and Developmental Standards for Four-Year-Olds. The screening measures—the Florida Kindergarten Readiness Screener (FLKRS)—are determined by the Department of Education by means of a competitive bid. Results from FLKRS are employed to calculate the VPK Provider Kindergarten Readiness Rate to measure how well a VPK provider prepares 4-year-old children to be ready for kindergarten, which is required by s. 1002.69(5), F.S.

From fall 2006 through fall 2008, FLKRS contained a subset of the Early Childhood Observation System(ECHOS) and the first two measures of the Dynamic Indicators of Basic Early Literacy Skills(DIBELS)(letter naming fluency and initial sound fluency) for kindergarten. For children whose mother tongue was Spanish, an alternative letter naming assessment was offered, that is Dinamincos Exito en la Lectura.

Starting from the 2009 - 2010 school year, FLKRS continued to involve a subset of ECHOS but replaced DIBELS with the Broad Screen and Broad Diagnostic Inventory, two measures from the Kindergarten Florida

Assessment for Instruction in Reading (FAIR-K). The Broad Screen consists of a phonemic awareness task and a letter naming task. The Broad Diagnostic Inventory includes a listening comprehension task and a vocabulary task. In the 2014 – 2015 school year, FLKRS was updated to contain the Work Sampling System, an observational tool, and the Kindergarten Florida Assessments for Instruction in Reading aligned to the Florida Standards (FAIR-FS).

Before the year of 2011, the readiness rate was calculated based upon the percentage of children ready on each measure. In the 2010 legislative session, s. 1002.69 (5), F.S., was amended to require children to be ready on both used measures (ECHOS and FAIR) to be considered ready for kindergarten. Regarding the 2010 – 11 VPK readiness rates, the State Board of Education used 70 as the minimum acceptable readiness rate for a VPK provider, referring that 70 percent of a provider's students who substantially finished the program screened ready on both ECHOS and FAIR. In the year of 2013, section 1002.69 (5), F.S., was revised to require the Office of Early Learning (OEL) to employ procedures to measure each VPK provider's kindergarten readiness rate. In the area of the 2012 – 13 readiness rates, OEL also adopted 70 percent as the minimum rate.

Pre-K in the State of Georgia

Georgia's Prekindergarten Program is a lottery funded educational program for Georgia's 4-year-old children to be ready for Kindergarten. Children who are four years old on September 1 of the current school year and who are Georgia residents are eligible to participate in Georgia's Pre-K Program during this school year. Georgia's Pre-K Program is voluntary for both families and providers.

Owing to the reason that participation in Georgia's Pre-K Program is voluntary for public schools and also for private child development centers, there may not be enough spaces in every district for all four year olds who wish to attend. Great efforts will be made to contract with eligible centers to offer enough spaces for children wishing to attend or to allocate children with available spaces in other Georgia's Pre-K Program providers in the district.

Georgia Lottery for Education

In spite of mounting evidence that high quality early education programs do improve children's development and chances of succeeding in school (Barnett, 1998), the nation's early care and education systems remain fragmented, underfunded, and insufficient to meet the needs of America's families (Kagan & Cohen, 1997). Over the last few years, as research affirming the importance of early development, particularly brain development, has begun to affect public policy debates (Shore, 1997), decision makers at all levels of government have been attaching importance to the availability and quality of early education. Some states have launched efforts to enhance early care and education as part of comprehensive early childhood initiatives. Others are expanding and promoting existing early education programs. Many states have determined to supplement federal Head Start funds to serve and assist more low-income children. Many more states are moving toward universal Prekindergarten, expanding their public school programs to include preschoolers (Mitchell, 1998). Because the system builds on an existing infrastructure, including relatively high standards and compensation for teachers, the Pre-K strategy seems to be gaining support across the nation.

In the 1990 gubernatorial election in Georgia, Governor Miller put forward the creation of the Georgia Lottery for Education. In order to ensure public support for the referendum, Governor Miller committed to the Georgia electorate that all funds would be made use of to supplement existing educational programs. He specifically favored the development of a college scholarship initiative and a preschool program. The voters of Georgia passed the proposal in November of 1992. Afterwards, he assigned senior staff in his Office of Planning and Budget, leaders of the Department of Education, and staff in the Department of Human Resources to formulate a plan for the preschool initiative.

Unlike the development and expansion of other statewide initiatives, formative hands-on management came directly from the Governor. Undoubtedly, the personal involvement of Governor Miller is clearly one of the most important reasons why a program serving a few hundred children at first has become big hit in the nation today.

The Pre-K Program started as a pilot program giving service to 750 at-risk four-year-old children and their families at around 20 sites in 1992. These programs were school-based, center-based, or home-based programs in accordance with individual community needs. Three million dollars from state funds afforded the program. In 1993 – 94, the first lottery funds were used to supply prekindergarten programs serving more than 8, 700 at-risk four-year-old children.

The next important prekindergarten milestone happened in September 1995 when the program was universally expanded to all eligible four-year-old children, instead of just at-risk families. The program tripled its expansion efforts from 15, 500 children in 1994 – 1995 to 44, 000 slots during the 1995 – 1996 school year. And the private sector turned to be an integral part of the program permitting the program to develop quickly without using funds for capital outlay on new buildings or facilities. A public and private partnership of this magnitude was a creative initiative in Georgia and the nation.

The Pre-K program continued to develop under the newly created Office of School Readiness from 57,000 children in 1996 – 1997 to 68,000 children in the 2003 – 2004 school year. Primary improvements in program quality, implementation of learning goals and quality standards, simplified administrative requirements, and intense training initiatives were put into practice. The instructional standards children enrolled in Pre-K were revised in 2003 to align with current research, and the program evaluation (Georgia's Pre-K Program Quality Assessment) was updated to help providers to raise the quality of services and meet the needs of the children. By the tenth anniversary of Georgia's Pre-K Program in 2002 – 2003, over 500,000 young children had attended the lottery funded Pre-K Program.

On July 1, 2004, the Office of School Readiness officially turned to Bright from the Start: Georgia Department of Early Care and Learning. The Department was started when the Georgia General Assembly approved Senate Bill 456 in the 2004 session. 72,000 children during the 2004 – 2005 school year participated in the Pre-K Program and 74,000 students during the 2005 – 2006 school year. A primary milestone was achieved during the 2009 – 2010 school year when the state became the first to serve more than one million young children in a voluntary, universal, lottery-funded program. In the 2010 – 2011 school year, more than 82,000 young children attended the program in every county in the state. In the 2012 – 2013 school year the program reached another milestone by celebrating the 20th anniversary of Georgia's Pre-K. In the 2012 – 2013 school year, the program served 84,000 children. The Department will carry on administering Georgia's Pre-K Program while fulfilling a comprehensive early care and education system. Georgia's Pre-K Program keeps updating policies and standards each year to improve quality services for children and families of Georgia.

Without the establishment of a lottery, Georgia could not have funded and carried out a large-scale Prekindergarten program. In order to understand how Georgia reached the forefront of early care and education policy, it is, therefore, of great significance to examine the components of Georgia's Pre-K Program.

Program Components

The program guidelines are comprised of the following components. The first one is eligible children. When initially envisioned, the program would mainly serve low-income four-year-old children. The program categorized "at-risk" children as those eligible for Medicaid, Aid to Families with Dependent Children (AFDC), the Women, Infants, and Children nutrition program (WIC), other child nutrition programs, or subsidized federal housing, or those referred by an agency serving children and families.

The second one is coordinating councils. The Early Childhood Division demanded the formation of local councils with the agencies involved in providing or coordinating services to children and families participating in the program. The Pre-K Advisory Committee placed a premium on creating community collaborations. Every council had to involve at least one parent of a child who was enrolled in the program and representatives from the agencies like the local Department of Family and Children Services, health department, and board of education. Pre-K sites were encouraged to involve representatives from other public and private agencies with their coordinating councils. The councils took the responsibility to develop the program application, to establish collaborations to supply available service to the children and families, and to develop and examine the program on an ongoing basis.

The third one is competitive open funding. Via a competitive process, all grants or contracts were about to be awarded to sites located in districts with an identified population of low-income children. It was required for applicators to demonstrate community need, like the percentage of families in the district below the poverty level and the number of children not served by existing preschool programs. Organizations eligible to apply for funding contained school systems, public and private non-profit agencies, and also private, for-profit child care providers. Coordinating councils were granted the authority to determine the most appropriate way to offer services to children and their families, either in homes, community settings or centers. The number of children served was limited to 12 in home settings. Classrooms and centers were regulated to have at least one teacher for every ten children and could not exceed 20 children.

In addition, DOE required that each program supply a local contribution to the funding of program. For the pilot program year(1992 – 1993), Georgia provided 70 percent of the funds, with a cost per child of about $ 4,000. Providers could realize their contribution through cash or, commonly, through in-kind services. Then, when lottery revenues became available, Georgia improved its share to 80 percent, with an average cost of $ 4,253 per child.

The fourth one is staffing. At first, personnel had to hold a high school diploma and working experience with children younger than five years old. The guidelines did not require providers to staff sites with certified teachers. Providers were encouraged, instead of being required, to select individuals with knowledge of child development, family dynamics and family needs, developmentally appropriate instructional practices, agencies and resources, and human diversity. Programs also could hire a parent educator, child and family development specialist, paraprofessional, who held a Child Development Associate (CDA) credential, certified teacher, special training in instruction of children younger than five, and an individual from other related fields with appropriate training or experience.

The fifth one is support services. Providers were required to provide basic health and developmental screenings; parent-focused services, including literacy, job training, and parent-education; and integrated access to mental health, drug treatment or crisis intervention programs if necessary. Beginning in the 1993 – 1994 year, DOE called for the adoption of Family Service Coordinators to offer targeted case management for families and to facilitate the coordination of needed services. To staff Family Service Coordinator position, programs had the option to hire a social worker/ case manager, community leader, counselor, health care worker, or mental health worker. In line with the program guidelines, the Family Service Coordinator would function as a multiple-service broker for the participating children and their families, coordinating opportunities for parents to attend educational or job-related programs. Each coordinator would implement home visits and assessments, carrying a maximum caseload of 40 families.

The sixth one is program length. Guidelines and funding formulas granted programs the flexibility to provide services of different length and intensity. The guidelines called for the consideration given to the integration of services which address the child care needs of working parents. While some districts offered half-day and traditional school-day services, many sites were funded to provide extended-day, and full-year programming. Programs were also required to offer transportation to families that needed such services.

From the outset, Georgia's Pre-K Program created a commitment to program evaluation. The Department of Education contracted with Georgia State University(GSU) to assesse the program's social and academic effects. Lorene(Quay) Pilcher and Marsha Kaufman-McMurrain from the GSU Department of Early Childhood Education completed a series of evaluations covering the early years of implementation. They evaluated the pilot program in 1992 – 1993 school year.

However, because Pre-K classes during the pilot year did not begin at the beginning of the school year, the researchers do not regard this evaluation as a rigorous assessment of the program's efficacy. In the first year of statewide implementation(1993 – 1994), researchers gathered a random sample of 317 Pre-K participants from 18 program sites geographically distributed throughout the state. After one year, when these children were completing kindergarten, 267 of them (84 percent) were located and compared to a randomly chosen matched group of 267 Pre-K-eligible students without participation in the Pre-K program. There were no significant differences found on the number of student referrals for special services or on measures of parents' attendance in the children's schooling. Overall, these results suggest that Prekindergarten significantly promoted the children's development and increased their chances for benefiting from kindergarten.

The achievement results suggest that Pre-K attendance had helped children academically. However, conforming to evaluations of many early intervention programs, the assessment showed that in the lack of consistent follow-through in the primary grades, lots of significant developmental gains tend to extinct over time. The fading of program effects provoked some concerns among Georgia educators and policy makers about the program efficacy during these early years of implementation.

Georgia Early Learning and Development Standards(GELDS)

Georgia has a long history as a leader in enhancing early learning and development outcomes for children. Georgia recently initiated its latest set of high-quality, research-based early learning standards for children birth through age five which is the Georgia Early Learning and Development Standards (GELDS). The GELDS expand quality learning experiences for children and address the question, "What should children know and be able to do from birth to age five?" The GELDS are a set of attainable, appropriate standards that are flexible enough to aid children's individual rates of development, cultural context, and approaches to learning. They are a continuum of skills, concepts, and behaviors that children fulfill throughout this time of life. They are divided into age groups and serve as a framework for learning. They are aligned with the Head Start

Child Outcomes Framework, the CCGPS for K-12, and the Work Sampling System Assessment.

The first of the National Education Goals articulates that all children will enter school ready to learn. Within the context of the nature of four-year-old children and how they learn, the State of Georgia has formulated a definition of school readiness. The state believes that school readiness must be defined within the context of families and how they live. It must be determined within the context of communities and the services they offer. Moreover, it must be defined within the context of schools and their readiness for children.

The major purposes of the GELDS are to instruct teachers who work with children from birth through five in offering quality learning experiences; instruct parents in supporting their children's development, growth, and learning potential; put the groundwork for using the standards in pre-service training, professional development, curriculum planning, and child outcome documentation; establish a universal language for all stakeholders to apply regarding the development and learning of children. Stakeholders would involve parents, teachers, pediatricians, early interventionists, policy-makers, and so on; arouse public awareness about the importance of the early years as the foundation for school achievement and lifelong learning and the significance of the teacher's role in the process; and aid the early identification and referral of children with special learning needs.

Pre-K in the State of Oklahoma

Oklahoma's universal Pre-Kindergarten program provides voluntary, free, school-based Pre-K to all 4 - year-old children in participating school districts. The program has a limitation of class size to 20 students and sets teacher-student ratios at 1-to-10. Oklahoma's Pre-K teachers are required to attain a bachelor's degree as well as childhood certification(NIEER-Barnett, 2013). In 2012 - 2013, state Pre-K programs expended an average of about $4,000 per student apart from federal and local funding, ranging from $1,300 to over $12,000 per student. Oklahoma spent $3,600 per Pre-K student(NIEER-Barnett, 2013). In line with improved academic outcomes, researchers suggest that increases in children's future earnings will exceed Oklahoma's costs; strongest income effects are projected for participants from low income families(Bartik, 2012; Brookings-Cascio, 2013).

Children, who are four years old on or before September 1, are eligible for the voluntary public school Pre-Kindergarten program. Currently, approximately 70% of Oklahoma's four-year-olds participate in public school and have access to the voluntary program. The program is funded by state general revenues. In addition, all funding flows through public schools and integrations with daycare centers and Head Start programs are possible. Oklahoma's universal Pre-K program has illustrated stronger effects for groups like Hispanics, blacks, and very poor children than for white and non-poor children(Gormley, 2005).

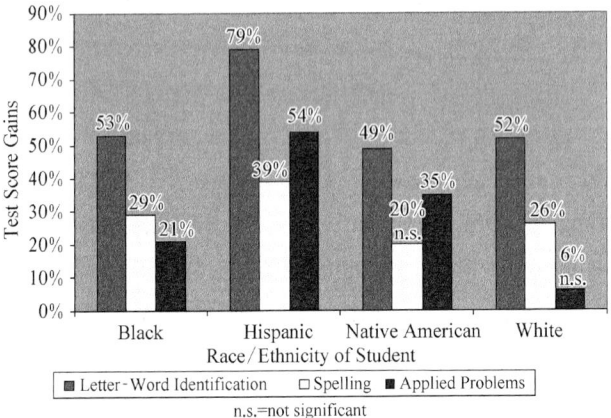

The chart comes from "The Effects of Oklahoma's Universal Pre-Kindergarten Program on School Readiness", written by William T. Gormley, Jr. in CROCUS and Georgetown University on June 18, 2007, p. 8.

Chart 4: Effects of Tulsa Pre-K Program by Race/Ethnicity of Student

Due to an early commitment to a voluntary universal pre-k system, Oklahoma has obtained national recognition for funding and establishing a comprehensive program. Legislation in 1990 funded pre-k beneficial for low-income children as a starting part of an education reform package largely emphasizing the K-12 level. Under the pre-k initiative, public schools had the option to participate in pre-k and receive state funding of about $1,000 per child (Preschool Yearbook, 2005). After preliminary results

Appendices

demonstrated gains for students attending the system, the state expanded universal voluntary pre-k in 1998 to any eligible four year-old child. With an enrollment of more than 30,000 children, the state now enrolls more than 60 percent of Georgia's four-year-olds in the program—a higher percentage of eligible youngsters than any other pre-k program nationwide(Gormley, Gayer, Phillips, & Dawson, 2004b).

Oklahoma's program is unique compared with other states because it operates entirely through the public schools. All pre-k teachers must hold a college degree and certification in early childhood education. And they receive the same salary as K-12 public school teachers and have wages considerably higher than their counterparts in Head Start and child care programs. Each pre-k class has no more than twenty children, with a child to staff ratio of 10:1. Individual districts can choose to provide half- or full-day service. In the year of 2003, fifty-six percent of pre-k programs operated for half-day. For the half-day programs, schools can integrate with Head Start and child care programs to offer additional child care and educational services.

The program is funded by the government through general education revenues with no dedicated pre-k line-item budget. And small to moderate budget increases, together with K-12 enrollment declines during the 1990s, permitted the state to fund universal pre-k system with minimal decreases to other education services. The state employs age and developmentally appropriate curriculum arranged with K-12 standards, and personnel must take part in continuing education. Ninety-four percent of local school districts have pre-k system.

Evaluations of the program have displayed significant positive effects. Georgetown University researchers inspected state-funded pre-k in Tulsa, the largest district in the state and also one of the most diverse (Gormley, Gayer, Phillips, & Dawson, 2004a). To examine children's gains that could be attributed to pre-k, the research compared recent pre-k graduates with children just about to start the program. The results showed that young children attending pre-k performed better than those with no participation of the program.

Comparison Between Mississippi and Other States

Early childhood education in the State of Mississippi is still in its starting stage. In 2013, Mississippi approved its first Pre-K law, the Early Learning Collaborative Act. In December of 2013, the first round of the Early Learning Collaborative award was offered to 11 different sites around the state. The major aim of the Early Learning Collaborative award is to supply funding to Early Learning Collaborative Councils to sustain and facilitate the realization of voluntary prekindergarten programs as identified in the Early Learning Collaborative Act of 2013.

Mississippi has long posed as a state that does not fund pre-k classes. Even though neighboring states have made great success in early education, Mississippi continues to be the only state in the South that doesn't establish voluntary prekindergarten programs. Researchers have found that high-quality pre-k programs do improve long-term outcomes for young children and assist to close an achievement gap for children who may worsen over time. Being able to listen to directions, stand in line, or have eye contact with the teacher play an primary role when it comes to teaching kids how to read and write. And a deficiency of school readiness is evident the moment children walk in on the first day of kindergarten.

All over the nation, about three-quarters of 4-year-olds participate in some type of public or private pre-k program. However, experts estimate that no more than half of Mississippi's 4-year-olds are in pre-k, and most of them are in federally funded Head Start programs targeting low-income families.

Preparing parents to call for access to high-quality preschools has proven to be a great challenge in Mississippi. Parents or grandparents who didn't participate in the program themselves may hardly see the value. The state's fragmented network of early childhood providers such as informal daycare, church-based programs, licensed facilities, and Head Start, refuses to always communicate with the public school system. Most of the programs do not have uniform quality standards. Moreover, to teach pre-k in Mississippi, teachers are only required to be 18 and hold a high school diploma or its equivalent.

For instance, teachers in Canton employ checklists, informal tests, and observational reports to track student progress, and they can even have their own criteria for holding children back. A great number of students have been struggling since 2010 when the state used the new Common Core standards for English and math, which supply parents and teachers with clear and concise expectations of what must be learned each grade. What's worse, the state is confronted with an even larger obstacle: getting rid of long-held attitudes about race. One out of every two black children in Mississippi lives in poverty, compared with 16 percent of white children, in accordance with the National Center for Children in Poverty.

The following chart (Chart 5) demonstrates the comparison between Mississippi and other states in early education.

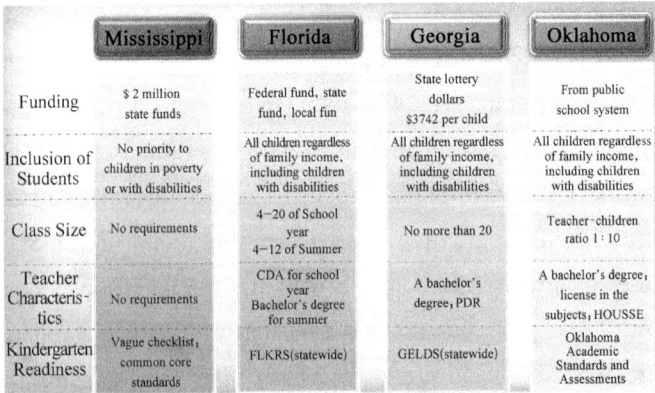

Chart 5: Comparison between MS and Other States

As a result, the State of Mississippi could draw on the experience of other states, like Florida, to impose voluntary prekindergarten program among small children who can benefit from the program. Also, Kindergarten Readiness Screener could be adopted to gather information about a child's overall development and address each student's readiness for kindergarten. Preschool children make the transition into kindergarten more successfully when their schools and families prepare for it together, and when their preschool and kindergarten teachers connect. In addition, by coordinating transition efforts, preschool and elementary programs can help children maintain and maximize the gains they made in preschool.

Recommendations for Prekindergarten in the State of Mississippi

On the basis of various resources of prekindergarten programs in other states, the State of Mississippi can draw on the experience in the following aspects, including establishment and expansion of statewide VPK, program funding, inclusion of students, class size, teacher characteristics, and kindergarten readiness.

Establishment and Expansion of Statewide Voluntary Prekindergarten Program

The State Department of Education can establish and

expand a statewide voluntary prekindergarten program. The program can be implemented step by step, starting by providing services for low-income children. Even though in 2013 the state legislature approved $3 million to fund voluntary pre-k programs, just six percent of 4-year-olds in Mississippi participate in a state-funded program. Data revealed that two-thirds of Mississippi's students begin kindergarten unprepared and hardly become proficient readers by third grades. A growing number of researches have demonstrated that high-quality pre-k programs do teach children important classroom skills, such as how to raise their hands and pay attention, as well as promote reading and math skills. In 2013, there were ten states that did not have voluntary preschool, while states like Florida and Oklahoma served more than 74 percent of their 4-year-olds in prekindergarten programs.

In 2004, the State of Florida imposed the Voluntary Prekindergarten Program (VPK). This legislation offers free prekindergarten services to all four-year-old children in the State of Florida. Florida carried out its VPK with the core goal of supplying high-quality preschool to young children to ensure all children would start kindergarten ready to learn. Some States, like Georgia and Florida, began their VPK by serving children of low socio-economic status and gradually expanded VPK to all four-year-old children, providing a free statewide universal prekindergarten program regardless of household income.

Funding

Prekindergarten funding of the State of Mississippi can come from federal funding, general state revenues (sales, income, property, taxes and fees by government), and local funding resources such as lottery money, gaming revenues and special dedicated taxes to satisfy the educational requirements of young children. In order to apply for federal funds for preschool, Mississippi must first improve the necessary infrastructure and capacity for scaling up a sustainable pre-k program.

In 1992, Georgia became the first state to implement a VPK for all four-year-old children regardless of the family's income, funded through state lottery dollars (Andrew & Slate, 2002; Henry, Henderson, Ponder, Gordon, Mashburn, & Rickman, 2003; SEF, 2007). Funding for the prekindergarten program came entirely from the state lottery dollars with an average two-year median cost from 2005 through 2006 of approximately $3910 per child. Providers from the public schools, private for-profit childcare centers, and not-for-profit childcare centers contracted with the Office of School Readiness to offer the prekindergarten program(Henry et al., 2006). Oklahoma was the next to follow with a statewide universal prekindergarten program in the late 1990's(Gormley et al., 2005; SEF, 2007). Funds for the prekindergarten program in Oklahoma came from the public school system. However, the funding per child in the State of Florida is one of the lowest in the Southern States.

Inclusion of Students

Mississippi's pre-k program can provide priority to low-income children and young children with disabilities and young children learning English are also included in the program.

In the State of Tennessee, low-income children are prioritized in its pre-k program. In the State of Florida, VPK has three options, school-year program, summer program, and specialized instructional services program. The specialized instructional services program is aimed to children with disabilities having current individual educational plans developed by local school districts. In these programs, certified or licensed professionals offer instruction in individual or small group settings.

Class Size

The class size of Mississippi's pre-k program can be limited to no more than twenty children in one classroom.

In the State of Florida, the class size is limited to no more than 20 students in school-year program and no more than 12 students in summer program. In the State of Georgia, the class size is limited to 10 children or a class size of no more than 20 with a teacher's assistance in the classroom. In the State of Oklahoma, the class size is limited to 20 children with a teacher to child ratio of one to ten. In small size class, children are more likely to attain more one-on-one attention, teachers can get to observe students better and better design lesson plans to satisfy each child's needs. With more engaging lessons and such personal attention, less class time is spent on addressing discipline and behavior problems. In addition, smaller classes can make a difference, especially when coordinated with other primary elements of a quality preschool program, like well-qualified teachers sensitive to students' needs and learning styles.

Teacher Characteristics

The State of Mississippi can increase education requirements and training for preschool teachers to enhance the quality of the individuals' preparation for their jobs (Mader, 2014). Preschool teachers must have a CDA credential or teaching certification in early childhood education and a bachelor's degree. The Child Development Associate Credential(CDA) is a nationally approved entry level credential in Early Childhood Education. It is issued by the Council for Professional Recognition. The CDA is designated for the individuals working with young children in all settings. And the CDA will prepare the potential preschool teachers to satisfy the specific needs of children and cooperate with parents and other adults to nurture children's physical, emotional, social, and intellectual growth in a child development framework. The CDA is a symbol of professionalism and affords assurance to parents and administrators that they have hired a competent teacher to work with their children.

The State of Florida requires teachers to have a CDA credential or teaching certification in early childhood education during the school year program and a bachelor's degree in early childhood education or a related field for summer program(Online Sunshine).

Kindergarten Readiness

The State of Mississippi can define statewide standards of kindergarten readiness and set up a statewide assessment system to evaluate the readiness of each child for kindergarten. The statewide, standardized assessment program will be designed and aligned to evaluate children's personal and social development, language and literacy, mathematical thinking, scientific thinking, physical development, health, and safety. Additionally, the assessment will specifically examine the development of children with special needs who are included in regular classrooms. Rather than supplying services to specific cultural or linguistic groups, the assessment program will also try to adopt inclusive or general language to align children from different cultural, linguistic, economic, and social backgrounds.

In the State of Florida, all kindergarten children receive a screening, regardless of whether the child participated in the VPK program, within the first 30 days of school (Florida Department of Education, 2016). The FLKRS is a screening instrument which employs two measurements. The first is the Early Childhood Observation System (ECHOS), which assesses a child's readiness to learn in a classroom environment (Florida Department of Education, 2016). The ECHOS screens children from kindergarten through second grade. The screen demonstrates what children can do within the classroom environment. The results of the ECHOS inform the teacher how to adopt individual instruction for each child. The tool aligns with national standards developed by some national associations throughout the United States (Smith, 2005). The second tool is the Broad Screen and Broad Diagnostic Inventory, two measures from the Kindergarten Florida Assessment for Instruction in Reading (FAIR-K). The Broad Screen consists of a phonemic awareness task and a letter naming task. The Broad Diagnostic Inventory includes a listening comprehension task and a vocabulary task. These measures are utilized to gather information about children's development in emergent reading.

References

Andrews, S. & Slate, J. (2002). Public and private prekindergarten programs: A comparison of student readiness. *Educational Research Quarterly*, 25 (3), 59-73.

Barnett, W. (1998). Long-term effects on cognitive development and school success. In *Early Care and Education for Children in Poverty*. Albany, NY: State University of New York Press.

Barnett, W., Carolan, M., & Squires, J. (2013). *The State of Preschool 2013: State preschool Yearbook*. New Brunswick, NJ: National Institute for Early Education Research(NIEER).

Bartik, T., & Lachowska, M. (2012). The short-term effects of the Kalamazoo Promise Scholarship on student outcomes. *W. E. Upjohn Institute for Employment Research*. 2012: 12-186.

Cascio, E., & Schanzenback, D. (2013). The impacts of expanding access to high-quality preschool education. *Brookings Papers on Economic Activity*. 1:127-178.

Florida Department of Education. (2016). *Florida Kindergarten Readiness Screener: State Report of District Results*. Retrieved June 13, 2016, from http://www.fldoe.org/earlylearning/pdf/flkrs-stdt-publicschools.pdf.

Gormley, W., Gayer, T., Phillips, D., & Dawson, B. (2004a). *The Effects of Oklahoma's Universal Pre-K on School Readiness*. Washington. DC: Georgetown University, Center for Research on Children in the U. S.

Gormley, W., Gayer, T., Phillips, D., & Dawson, B. (2004b). *The Effects of Universal Pre-K on Cognitive*

Development. Washington. DC: Georgetown University, Center for Research on Children in the U. S.

Gormley, J., Gayer, T., Phillips, D., & Dawson, B. (2005). The effects of universal Pre-K on cognitive development. *Developmental psychology*, 41(6), 872 - 884.

Gormley, W., & Philips, D. (2005). The effects of universal Pre-K in Oklahoma: Research highlights and policy implications. *Policy Studies Journal*, 2005, 33 (1): 65 - 82.

Henry, G. T., Gordon, C. S., & Rickman, D. K. (2006). Early education policy alternatives: comparing quality and outcomes of Head Start and state prekindergarten. *Educational Evaluation and Policy Analysis*, 28(1), 77 - 97.

Henry, G. T., Henderson, L. W., Ponder, B. D., Gordon, C. S., Mashburn, A. J., & Rickman, D. K. (2003). *Report of the findings from the early childhood study: 2001 - 02*. Retrieved June 17, 2008, from http://aysps. gsu. edu/publications/2003/earlychildhood. pdf.

Kagan, S, & Cohen, N. (1997). *Not by Chance: Creating an Early Care and Education System for America's Children*. New Haven: Bush Center for Child Development and Social Policy.

Mader, J. (2014). State loses out on preschool funding— again. *The Hechinger Report*. Retrieved December 17, 2014, from http://www. jacksonfreepress. com/news/ 2014/dec/17/state-loses-out-preschool-fundingagain/

Mitchell, A. (1998). Prekindergarten programs funded by the states: essential elements for policy makers. Reports published on *Families and Work Institute Web Site*.

Online Sunshine. (2016). *The 2016 Florida statutes* (Chapter 1002). Retrieved from http://www.leg.state.fl.us/Statutes/index.cfm?App_mode = Display_Statute&URL = Ch1002/ch1002.

Shore, R. (1997). *Rethinking the Brain: New Insights into Early Development, Families and Work Institute*. New York.

Smith, S. (2005). Successfully guiding early learning. *Harcourt Assessment Happenings*. Retrieved June 12, 2008, from http://harcourtassessment.com/hai/images/dotcom/echosonline/happenings.pdf.

Southern Education Foundation. (2007). *Pre-Kindergarten in the south: The region's comparative advantage in education*. Retrieved May 15, 2008, from www.southerneducation.org.

Appendix H: Dissertation Evaluation

The source of the dissertation is Markova-Lama, I. (2013). *Effects of academic and non-academic instructional approaches on preschool ELLs' English language development* (Doctoral dissertation). Retrieved from ProQuest Dissertations and Theses. (Accession Order No. UMI 3587354).

Title of the Dissertation

The title of this study is *Effects of academic and non-academic instructional approaches on preschool ELLs' English language development*, the frame of which is so straightforward and uncomplicated that the readers of the dissertation can easily get aware of the research concept and methods. This title is brief with no waste of words like unnecessary articles and prepositions. And the focus of the study is included in it.

Abstract

The central issue of this study was to explore whether English language learners in preschool would engage more and practice more in English during academic or non-academic instructional activities and also to examine the perceptions of preschool teachers and parents of ELLs about the effects of academic and non-academic activities upon student engagement and their English language development.

The researcher employed both quantitative and qualitative research methods in this study, in which the participants included eight preschool ELLs, twelve preschool teachers, and eight parents of these bilingual children. Data sources consisted of 285 preschool observations, teacher and parent interviews, and teacher and parent surveys.

The findings revealed that ELLs in preschool engaged and interacted dramatically more in non-academic classroom activities than in academic activities. And the findings from teacher and parent surveys and interviews indicated that both teachers and parents perceive non-academic classroom activities as being more beneficial to young ELLs' engagement and English language development than academic activities.

The major implication of this study is that non-academic preschool classroom activities may be more beneficial in developing preschool bilingual children's English language skills than academic activities. In addition, the importance of non-academic activities might extend beyond preschool classroom setting, and the researcher highly recommends that more non-academic social-based activities for bilingual students be implemented in K-12 classrooms in order to promote their English language development.

The Problem Statement

The researcher stated the problem logically and clearly by providing a brief literature review at the very beginning and linking the problem to the title of the dissertation. The research problem is to investigate which instructional approaches, academic and non-academic, benefit preschool bilingual learners in attaining English language proficiency and help to identify the most efficient classroom activities for preschool ELLs.

In terms of the purpose of the study, there are two major purposes, one of which is to examine the engagement level and English language use of eight preschool ELLs during academic and non-academic classroom activities. The second purpose is to approach twelve preschool teachers and eight parents and investigate their perceptions of the effects of academic and non-academic instructional approaches on preschool ELLs' English language development.

This study studied the following research questions: (1) What is the effect of free-play activities on second language(L2) development of bilingual preschool children? (2) What is the effect of teacher-structured time activities on L2 development of bilingual preschool children? (3) What are the preschool teachers' perceptions of the effect of free-play vs. teacher-structured activities on the English language development of bilingual preschool children? (4) What are the preschool parents' perceptions of the effect of free-play vs. teacher-structured activities on the English language development of bilingual preschool children(Markova-Lama, 2013)? It can be figured out from these questions that they logically describe responses to different variables and share the same pattern of word order, which enables readers to easily attain the main variables (Creswell, 2014).

Also, the final section included a brief and explicit explanation of a large number of terms which might be unacquainted with the readers, including approaches to learning, bilingual child, child-centered approach, cognitive competence, circle time, didactic approach, early childhood setting, English language learners, expressive language, language pragmatics, preschool teacher, pretend play, receptive language, social competence, social conventions, social learning theory, utterance, , and zone of proximal development.

Review of Literature

The literature review was broken into several subtopics, involving SLA during preschool years, preschool curriculum, child-centered approach, teacher-structured approach, mixed approach, classroom engagement, teacher perceptions, and parent perceptions. These points seemed to adequately outline a comprehensive approach to the identified area of study. And the cited sources in these subtopics are pertinent to the study. The existing literature covered the latest studies related to this study, which provided with a larger, ongoing dialogue in the literature and called for the needs of this study to fill in gaps and extend prior studies (Marshall & Rossman, 2011). The literature review was generally shaped from the large research problem to the narrow issues which allowed for easy understanding of the readers in the methods of this study. Additionally, the researcher held a neutral position in selecting the sources. Nevertheless, the researcher also put forward the limitations of some studies in that these studies are based primarily on the examination of two instructional approaches. As a result, the study on comparison between the two approaches that the researcher has completed, to a great extent, was researchable and necessary.

Design and Procedures

Chapter Three was methodology, in which qualitative and quantitative methods were both validated in order to increase the reliability of the study. This study is an original study which described the research method thoroughly, starting by pointing out the respective data collection to answer the four research questions. The instruments used in the study were comprised of two versions of survey for teachers and parents, *Preschool Teacher Literacy Beliefs Questionnaire* (Hindman & Wasik, 2008), *Teacher Belief Scale* (Charlesworth et al., 1991), and the researcher herself. In observation and interviews, the researcher was the instrument in collecting and analyzing data. Owing to a purposeful homogeneous sampling method, eight preschool ELLs, twelve preschool teachers, and eight parents participated in the study.

The independent variable for all of the four research questions was preschool classroom activity. This dichotomous variable consists of two subcategories: academic and non-academic preschool classroom activities. The dependent variable for the first and second research questions was English language development, as measured by both the children's level of engagement in academic and non-academic preschool classroom activities and their language use including progress in these activities. The dependent variable for the third research question was preschool teachers' perceptions of the effects that academic and non-academic activities had on ELLs' English language development. The dependent variable for the fourth one was parents' perceptions of the effects that academic and non-academic activities had on their preschool children's

English language development.

Data Analysis and Presentation

When it comes to the data analysis, the researcher adopted preschool classroom observations, surveys, teacher interviews, and parent interviews in the process of data collection. In classroom observations, both qualitative and quantitative data were used to examine bilingual students' engagement level and language use. Children's scores were analyzed by normative scales by converting raw scores into z-scores. And field notes were qualitatively analyzed and divided into several themes through a coding process. In surveys, the quantitative data were collected and then analyzed by SPSS software (George & Mallery, 2011) with descriptive statistics, including frequency, percentage, means, and standard deviations. In interviews, the qualitative data were transcribed and coded into diverse categories and then themes.

The findings from observations responded to research questions one and two, which indicated that English language learners in preschool had a higher level of engagement and English language use during non-academic classroom activities than in academic ones. What is more, the findings from surveys and interviews provided answers to research questions three and four, which revealed that the majority of teachers and parents perceived non-academic activities more beneficial to children's English language development than academic activities. Overall, the findings supported the research purpose and resolved the research questions.

Conclusions and Implications

Chapter five informed the readers the discussion of the findings, limitations, delimitations, implications, recommendations for future research. The purpose of the study was to find out which preschool classroom activities, academic or non-academic activities, exert greater effects on preschool ELLs' English language development, which was discussed in detail in conclusions from a variety of perspectives.

Preschool educators, policy makers, and future research can attain a number of recommendations from this study. For the preschool educators, they can receive training on the importance of non-academic activities, implement more non-academic activities in class, adopt different terminology in unstructured time, set shorter time for specific non-academic activities without interrupting peer-to-peer interactions, create new non-academic activities and play areas for children, and so on. For the policy makers, they can promote more non-academic activities in preschools, make it mandatory for young ELLs to attend two years of preschool, and launch two levels of preschool: three-to-four years old children and four-to-five years old children. For the future research, the researcher can collect data from a larger sample group to increase the generalizability of the results, study on teacher or parent intervention programs beneficial to bilingual children's English language development, and investigate the effectiveness of teachers' attitudes and strategies in bilingual children's English language development.

APA Format

The dissertation follows most of APA format guidelines in the main sections, the nuts and bolts of styles like spacing, punctuation, page layout, spelling, margins, capitalization, abbreviations, numbers, statistics, the use of graphic elements, and reference citation. However, the format of the title page is inconsistent with the APA guideline, which lacks the running head.

Overall Assessment

To sum up, this dissertation is well organized with the research problem, review of literature, methodology, findings, and discussion and recommendations. The considerations in this dissertation with regard to selection of the participants, logical interpretation of the findings, and the careful management of the biased data boost the reliability and validity of the study. Admittedly, this dissertation contributed much to my project in that it provided an overall literature review of preschool bilingual children's English language development and a model of research methodology. However, even though the mixed-approach design has broader perspectives and uses the strengths of both methodologies, it is hard for me to handle this time-consuming, complex research process which requires efficient interpretation of conflicting results and analysis of both qualitative and quantitative data.

References

Charlesworth, R., Hart, C. H., Burts, D. C., & Hernandez, S. (1991). Kindergarten teachers beliefs and practices. *Early Child Development and Care,* 70(1), 17–35.

Creswell, J. W. (2014). *Research design: Qualitative, quantitative, and mixed methods approaches,* (4th Edition). SAGE Publications, Incorporated.

George, D., & Mallery, P. (2011). *SPSS for Windows step by step: A simple guide and reference* 18.0 Update, 11th Edition. Boston, MA: Pearson Publication.

Hindman, A. H., & Wasik, B. A. (2008). Head Start teachers' beliefs about language and literacy instruction. *Early Childhood Research Quarterly,* 23(4), 479–492.

Markova-Lama, I. (2013). *Effects of academic and non-academic instructional approaches on preschool ELLs'*

English language development (Doctoral dissertation). Retrieved from ProQuest Dissertations and Theses. (Accession Order No. UMI 3587354).

Marshall, C., & Rossman, G. B. (2011). *Designing qualitative research* (5th ed.). Thousand Oaks, CA: Sage.